DATE DUE

PRINTED IN U.S.A.

Helping HoardersA Guide for Families, Counselors, and First Responders

by Mark A. Chidley, LMHC, Certified Rapid
Resolution Therapist

Table of Contents

Introduction

As I completed the first draft of an article about hoarding that would later be published in **Counseling Today**, I desired to have my daughter Margaret, whose editorial skills far outmatch mine, read over the article and give me her feedback. In the course of doing that she shared my project with a colleague in her advertising agency. This young, up and coming creative writer in the agency immediately asked permission to contact me and get a consult about a hoarding situation in his own family, which was reaching its critical point. He was at his wits end, as were his siblings, dealing with a mother whose hoarding had gone on for decades. A year later, while attending a Rapid Resolution Therapy training (an innovative trauma therapy created by Dr. Jon Connelly), I was astonished that several other therapists insisted on taking me aside during lunch and hearing what I had to say about treating hoarders. Several of them had either a current client or an affected friend or family member whose hoarding difficulties had touched their lives, and they were hungry for information on what worked with this often perplexing population.

So it began to dawn on me that even with the notoriety and nationwide attention given the subject by the popular television series on A&E, and the appearance of some good literature, that many people were still in need of a concise way of understanding the disorder and a grasp of the steps of a helpful approach. Hoarding has come out of the closet. People who had been trying on their own to put the pieces together are joining others who have an increased interest in the disorder and, whether lay or professional, want to be part of the conversation and bring up their skills to effectively address it. They want to be better equipped in dealing with a problem that, truly, is often found right in our own backyard.

In writing this book I am not trying for a lengthy treatise, but rather a pocket guide. I've assembled my own experience along with some of the best material that has come out over the last few years, as a digest, written in plain language that can be read through and assimilated relatively quickly. I'm thinking of the social worker out there, who has been called into a hoarder's situation with little previous background, or the worried family member who wants to approach it knowledgeably in order to do their best. My hope is that this little book will make the subject more accessible to a wider audience and serve as a springboard for future learning and experience. I especially hope, as with that young man mentioned above, that any whose heart has been troubled or patience stretched by the prolonged crisis that hoarding is, may herein find a light as they proceed forward.

— Mark Chidley, August, 2011

Author's Note

Cases described in this book are either shared with clients' permission or are representative of typical client stories. Some stories have been combined and names or other identifying details have been changed to protect privacy.

Although this book offers tools to help you deal with a hoarder, it is not a substitute for professional help. Please contact your local Task Force on Hoarding, Animal Control, or Public Health Department. They may suggest a qualified mental health professional in your area if you need additional support.

For my mother, Virginia, my father, William, and my brother, Bill

When Jesus came by, he looked up at Zacchaeus and called him by name. "Zacchaeus!" he said. "Quick, come down! I must be a guest at your home today." Zacchaeus quickly climbed down and took Jesus to his house in great excitement and joy. But the people were displeased. "He has gone to be the guest of a notorious sinner, "they grumbled.

— Luke 19: 5

I. Get Your Own Mind Right First

Not too long ago I was sitting in the production studio at WGCU, our local public radio station, with two recovering hoarders. We three were being interviewed for a noontime show. I was listening to their answers as our host, Valerie Edwards, asked them what it had been like to be "discovered" as a hoarder and what led them to accept help and begin to get well. Both gave their own versions of essentially the same answer: it was in the non-judgmental attitude of the first person through the door combined with a legitimate offer to help. A hoarder has usually been living in secret, going to lengths to avoid scrutiny, burdened with shame, fear, and possibly resentment of family, neighbors, or the authorities. To approach with respect and sensitivity to their being, already overwhelmed by the problem, is like a breath of fresh air for a hoarder. It is what makes all the difference of whether you can proceed or not. Adam Leath, a friend of mine who heads daily operations for Animal Control, has this attitude down pat. It can be as simple as the offer of extra kitty litter or a bag of pet food passed to a person through a tentatively cracked door. Adam usually gets himself invited in on his first visit because he quickly demonstrates he is there to help and not judge. The attitude Adam embodies actually has three components, which I will break down in the following paragraphs: Compassion, Curiosity, and Patience.

Compassion

Compassion comes from really getting inside various hoarders' stories either through reading or experience. The uninformed public's view is extreme and skewed. Hoarders are thought to be just lazy, dirty, crazy, or all three. Hoarders are people who have become overwhelmed by a disorder of thought, emotion, and behavior they don't understand. Except for those in extreme denial in the later stages, most are just as confused and confounded by their predicament as anyone. And most of them, approached in the right way, will be responsive to the offer of help. One lady especially comes to mind. She came by way of referral from a mental health court diversion program. She had amassed an unusual amount of cheap items, mostly through compulsive shoplifting. These items were spread throughout most of her home and into the garage. At the end of my first visit, as we walked to the door, she confessed she was feeling a huge sense of relief. "Why?" I asked.

"Because you treated me with respect. I spent all afternoon worrying about you showing up, thinking that you would take a look at all this and think I was a terrible person."

For years hoarders have been told (or told themselves) they are slobs, losers, and out of control misfits not fit to live among others. Please keep this social injury in the back of your mind along with their loss of a sense of common humanity. I recommend preparing for the visit in the following way: take a moment and look back on one of your own failures or a time you blew it. Now think of the response of one person who made all the difference for you, who took the trouble to understand. If you do this before you go, you will automatically respond in the best possible way and be miles ahead of others in forming a connection.

Curiosity

Shame plays such a huge role in a hoarder's outlook. It's the reason most of them keep the blinds drawn or talk through a cracked door, rather than run the risk of the outside world looking in and judging them. The second element, curiosity, the right kind of curiosity, comes in as an attitude that can counter and start to diffuse the intense shame that rules a hoarder's life. I remember the first hoarding scene in which I participated and how I was called to handle the wrong kind of curiosity.

Animal Control called and requested my assistance at a home in a nearby community in which they found 77 cats. The call had originated with a neighbor complaining about the odor coming from the home. When I arrived there were three police squad cars, four Animal Control vans, and other cars that belonged to city and county code enforcement. Several neighbors were standing out in their driveways, and the one who had placed the complaint had her home movie camera set up on a tripod. It had all the makings of a spectacle, which the minute the hoarder stepped out of her doorway, would likely doom our chances of gaining her cooperation on that day. I immediately veered toward the lady with the camera. I explained the delicate nature of what we were about to attempt and our earnest need for her full cooperation in not drawing undue attention or filming. I explained Animal Control's Public Information Officer would keep her posted. She readily complied, and both she and her neighbors went inside.

The right kind of curiosity could be characterized as what's referred to in Zen as Beginner's Mind. Whoever shows up first has to be willing to be taught to get to know the hoarder as a person. Letting them reveal at their own pace, I can usually pick up a thread or theme or bit of information that might break the ice or later be helpful. The essential phrase taught to me in my Rapid Resolution training was, "I don't want to understand by knowing how I would feel, but to really understand how it's been for you." This phrase, along with some Motivational Interviewing tools, which will be discussed later, can open the hoarder up to the possibility of trusting in a relationship with an actual person, as opposed to the relatively safe animals and objects they've substituted.

In their book *Digging Out*, (Tompkins and Hartl) the authors note there is all the difference in the world between the question, "Why do you have this?" and, "Why do you have this, here." The first puts the hoarder on the defensive. The second shows curiosity about placement and avoids justification for having the object in the first place. As the hoarder answers, the helper gains all sorts of valuable information about how they think about their habitat and how they assign importance to various locations throughout the house. The word here is just one little word, one small emphasis, but the attitude of curiosity and joining the hoarder in his or her world comes through loud and clear.

Patience

As you read your way into the published literature, and surely as you gain experience, the value of patience becomes abundantly clear. This is something the TV shows, in their limited timeframe to tell a compelling story quickly, sometimes omit. Most hoarding situations don't clear up in 48 minutes or even 48 hours. It's not uncommon to have friends, relatives, and agency visitors preparing the groundwork for whatever change can be made for a year or more before it actually occurs. You have to hold in mind a target, which the hoarder can realistically attain, and hold to it despite day-to- day steps forward or backward. Of course, the exception to this is any kind of forced intervention, such as by public health, coding, animal control, or police. In that instance, the rules change. These will be discussed briefly in a bit. But by and large, a huge dose of patience will never hurt you. Hoarders can sense when others are pushing their own agendas and are acutely sensitive to interpersonal pressure. If you are the kind of helper whose self-esteem rests on quickly getting someone else to do the right thing (called the righting reflex), then I will tell you ahead of time, you've met your match. Hoarders are notoriously resistant to outside pressure, and strongly reinforced by their own avoidance to defer emotional discomfort by doing more of what they've been doing, sometimes despite severe consequences.

What appears as stubbornness is born of an inflexibility of mind and fear of change that work together to their disadvantage. When hoarders get a thought in their head and sense others would like to change it, they are likely to stand their ground and cling to it all the more. There are two traps to avoid here, called The Expert Trap and the Premature Focus Trap. If you come across as having all the answers to questions the hoarder is not yet asking, or even ready to face, or, if you predetermine the agenda, pushing for things on which the hoarder is not yet ready to focus, you can fall into these traps. I know; I've had to climb out of them a time or two, myself.

Better to offer your idea on a take it or leave it basis, first asking their permission to share a thought, and timing your delivery carefully. What makes for good timing? Wait for when the context makes the idea all the more relevant, or, the hoarder is in a good space, relatively more relaxed and open to hear it. This minimizes the odds of tripping a hoarder into an emotional defense of his or her position, a mistake family members often make. Unfortunately, once this happens, the level of resistance will increase exponentially and might stay there for a while, lengthening the process. Hoarders are known for just shutting down and either retreating to their rooms or ordering everyone out when they get frustrated.

It is all an exaggerated version of what occurs with most of us. We all like our freedom to choose and determine how we will live. We all react when we feel someone is trying to control us. Hoarders are the same, but with a much shorter fuse and much higher level of distortion. Sometimes they believe they are fighting for the last shreds of their dignity against a world they imagine would like to strip it away from them. You can see, then, how patience, and reminding yourself that the hoarder is still ultimately the one responsible to be causative in his or her own life, are key assets to take along.

II. Get to Know What Hoarding Is

Though it's a centuries-old phenomenon, hoarding has only been studied by researchers and mental health experts in the last twenty years or so. We are very late in coming to the party. Stereotypes, stigma, and misunderstanding have been the rule, not the exception.

The currently accepted definition of object hoarding is just now being crafted by a study group within the American Psychiatric Association. It will likely be published in the Fifth Edition of the *Diagnostic and Statistical Manual of Mental Disorders*, due to come out in 2013. It reads as follows:

Hoarding is characterized by

A. Persistent difficulty discarding or parting with possessions, regardless of their value

B. This difficulty is due to strong urges to save items and/or distress associated with discarding

C. The symptoms result in the accumulation of a large number of possessions that fill up and clutter active living areas of the home or workplace to the extent that their intended use is no longer possible. If all living areas are uncluttered, it is only because of the interventions of third parties (e.g., family members, cleaners, authorities)

D. The symptoms cause clinically significant distress or impairment in social, occupational, or other important areas of functioning (including maintaining a safe environment for self and others)

E. The hoarding symptoms are not due to a general medical condition (e.g. brain injury, cerebrovascular disease)

F. The hoarding symptoms are not restricted to the symptoms of another mental disorder (e.g., hoarding due to obsessions in Obsessive-Compulsive Disorder, decreased energy in Major Depression, delusions in

Schizophrenia or another Psychotic Disorder, cognitive deficits in Dementia, restricted interests in Autism Spectrum Disorder, food storing in Prader-Willi Syndrome).

The person evaluating the hoarding is to specify if the behavior appears with **Excessive Acquisition**, and with what **Level of Insight** the hoarder appears to be functioning on a continuum of Good, Fair, Poor, or Absent. Excessive Acquisition is defined as excessive collecting, buying, or stealing of items that are not needed or for which there is no available space.

There is a lot in this to digest. I often get asked by people trying to understand the disorder if their cherished collection of sports memorabilia or their mom's penchant for certain lipsticks or the closet full of clothes they've held onto, or the fact that they've kept all their report cards and awards since first grade makes them a hoarder. The answer is no, unless you qualify under criteria B, C, and D. Many people collect things, go through fads, hang onto keepsakes, or create inventories in order to sell or trade items. These traits are not hoarding. We all have a junk drawer at home or an area that could use a little tidying up from time to time. Only when use of one's living spaces is rendered impossible (a junk drawer turns into a junk room), and there develops the significant distress parting with objects and the impairment of other life activities, do you have hoarding.

The APA criteria may seem a little complex and hard to grasp at first, but reading between the lines you pick up on the massive breakdown of good judgment that develops with hoarding, which you will experience the minute you set foot in a hoarder's home. Their distress is relative to level of insight. Hoarders with less insight tend to show less distress. Distress manifests as life becomes unlivable or a crisis occurs or there is pressure to change from others. Also, a person can hoard without excessively acquiring, by simply refusing to discard or let anything leave the home. All these unique features set it apart from other disorders.

And we're reminded in this new definition to rule out the other medical or psychological conditions that have some (but not all) features of hoarding behavior which by their presence would better account for it. For instance, several years ago while working for Hospice, I went into homes of single, adult patients who were dealing with a stroke or a progressive dementia or were just too weak from a terminal illness to attend to housekeeping. Things had piled up, with almost as much chaos as in hoarding cases, but this clearly was not a hoarder or due to a lifelong pattern of hoarding.

Hoarders experience impairment in what are called their ADL's, Activities of Daily Living. They may not attend to their hygiene, cook a meal, or invite friends over because the spaces are now filled with stuff, which blocks the use of the rooms for their associated purposes. They might not be able to find their checkbook or other important papers in the mounting piles of clutter, and so get behind on their bills or lose track of other important commitments or deadlines.

As an illustration, I remember being a home health aide, working my way through school. I got assigned to a retired orthodox priest who in his later years had been a part-time university professor and a full-time information junkie. His little apartment was packed out, turned into part museum, part library. Books, journals, and academic memorabilia were everywhere, including stacked in the refrigerator as well as over, under, and all around the toilet. Getting a nutritious meal into him posed a major challenge because he would bring home sliced meat, oranges, cheese, and other things he liked. Then he'd leave them out on top of the counter because there was no room left in the refrigerator. By the time of my weekly visit, the food had usually spoiled and had to be tossed. His pet academic interest was literally more important to him than eating or being able to go to the toilet, which was evidenced by his possession of every bit of information ever published on the topic. Often, I had to firmly urge him to undress and let me run a load of laundry while I was there because all his clothes, including those on his back, had been soiled and reused over and over without washing. You guessed it, because his washer and dryer were filled with papers and books.

Homes deteriorate if appliances, utilities, wiring, and plumbing are not repaired regularly. Walls and floors can deteriorate from within if piles of stuff mix with moisture and set up mold. The hoarder's quality of life may therefore start to nosedive and health risks increase sharply. The hoard may even pose an imminent danger of fire, injury (if the piles are high and in danger of falling), disease, respiratory problems, or infection. These latter risks come from the infestations of rats, mice, roaches, and other vermin which can transmit diseases through their droppings or saliva, as they take up residence and multiply quickly in a severe hoarding situation.

So far we've just discussed objects. The rate of deterioration, impairment, distress, and danger to health (not to mention impact on others) accelerates even more dramatically when animals are thrown into the equation. Animal hoarding is defined by:

A. Failure to provide minimum standards of space, sanitation, nutrition, and veterinary care for animals

B. The inability to recognize the effects of this failure on the welfare of animals, humans, the household, and the environment.

C. Obsessive attempts to accumulate or collect animals in the face of deteriorating conditions.

D. Denial or minimization of problems and living conditions.

There are three subtypes of animal hoarders: The Overwhelmed Caregiver, the Rescue Hoarder, and the Exploiter Hoarder.

Overwhelmed Caregivers are typically animal lovers who got overextended, took in too many, and now can't manage. They tend to have more insight, more genuine concern for their animals, and are more cooperative with authorities and helpers.

Rescue Hoarders have a strong sense of mission to protect animals from euthanasia or reproductive control, are more active in their acquisition of animals, and much less cooperative with authorities. They may pose as rescuing to provide adoption, but this will ultimately turn out to be a rescue-only pattern, as they believe themselves to be the only ones capable of providing the proper care.

Exploiter Hoarders are the most difficult to engage because they lack empathy or respect for either animals or humans. They have extreme control needs and acquire animals because they need to dominate something. They tend toward extreme denial of the cruelty and neglect their animals suffer, often exhibit hostility, and typically reject all authority or attempts to help. They believe themselves superior to all others as far as animals are concerned. They are sociopathic con artists and have even been known to set up cover foundations or give interviews as self-acknowledged experts, cannily misrepresenting positions of government officials to build their own case or prestige to the media. Even after being incarcerated or fined, these hoarders usually just reset their operation in a new jurisdiction or with new layers of camouflage. The only way to finally stop an Exploiter Hoarder may be lengthy jail time or if something such as a medical illness intervenes to incapacitate them and put them out of business.

Assessment and Impact

70% of the time, the typical animal hoarder is a female, over 65, alone, and often socioeconomically disadvantaged. Object hoarders break down roughly 50% male and female, respectively. Recent studies put the prevalence rate of hoarding between 2%-5% of the general population. This translates into somewhere between 6-15 million Americans affected by some form of hoarding disorder. In a county the size of the one I live in, 600,000, it translates to between 12,000-30,000 cases, numbers that stun attendees at our Task Force's seminars and make a cold shiver run down the spines of county department heads.

Each case can run into hundreds of hours of time invested in inspections and monitoring for safety and compliance, and social service resourcing. Cleaning, temporary housing, and restoration of a property to minimum standards can run into the thousands of dollars and involve the coordination of multiple agencies before it's all through. An advanced, deteriorated hoarder in a home that requires either full-scale demolition or total renovation can cost up to $100,000.

Presently, such interventions of time and money come straight out of the working budgets of existing agencies and county departments. Even with special housing assistance programs that kick in under emergency conditions, it doesn't take a math whiz to ascertain that no city or county could sustain this for long. The number of cases cited above is not going to be manifest at the same time. Most are hidden, in some stage of their development, for reasons described below.

At the end of the day, hoarding presents in varied forms as a mostly hidden, evolving disorder, making it frustratingly hard to measure and not readily translatable into definite statistical or cost categories. The person may be young or old, single or married, living alone or in a family—white collar, blue collar, rich or poor, or anything in between. Object hoarding can be a separate phenomenon from animal hoarding or the two can overlap once animals are present. All cases eventually affect someone else, and at some point the whole community pays the bill, not just the financial one, but the emotional one, too, as we wrestle with the stress, human anguish, and consternation that is hoarding.

Hoarders are unusually adept at restricting access to their lifestyle. This is because their denial, shame, and resistance to help synchs with societal values on privacy and self-determination. The Fourth Amendment of the Constitution protects us all against unnecessary search and seizure of property, goods, personal effects and papers. Officials can't just drop by and inspect unless they have probable cause to suspect harm. These factors work together so that hoarders are most often discovered only after they've been at it awhile, sometimes decades. They draw the blinds, shutter their windows, and talk to visitors through the door, careful to prevent viewing of the inside. While visitors may note the odd behavior, most won't suspect the true situation on the other side of the door, and usually don't see anything amiss from the outside or casually driving by. That is, unless the hoard is late stage four or five and it has spilled out of the house into cars, carports or yard areas.

Hoarding scenarios are ranked on a continuum of 1-5 stages. One of the most commonly accepted tools was developed by the National Study Group on Chronic Disorganization (NSGCD) and can be downloaded from their website: http://www.challengingdisorganization.org/. It ranks situations in an ascending scale of severity, and within each level, the four factors of Structure and Zoning, Pets and Rodents, Household Functions, and Sanitation and Cleanliness are evaluated.

The Clutter Image Rating Scale developed by the OCD Foundation is a nice visual accompaniment to the NSGCD tool http://www.ocfoundation.org/hoarding/. Take a moment and familiarize yourself with these, so you will be able to form a mental picture of what is meant when you hear a hoarding situation rated on the 1-5 scale.

Bear in mind these scales look at the hoarder's home and do not rate the hoarder's state of mind, physical condition or other needs. The HOMES Multi-disciplinary Risk Assessment and the Structured Interview for Hoarding Disorder are two such tools. The HOMES tool is briefer, meant for any responder, and can be accessed at https:// www.masshousing.com.

The Structured Interview for Hoarding Disorder (SIHD) is geared toward clinicians and found at the OCD Foundation website listed above. Finally, The Hoarding Severity Scale and Activities of Daily Living Scale were developed by Dr. Randy Frost and his associates, and also add biopsychosocial features. The Frost tool is in the book **Buried in Treasures**, listed in the Sources section. Taken together, these begin to provide a common language to gauge the severity of the hoarder's situation.

Possible Origins

A final piece of the puzzle comes from theories on hoarding's causes. With only the first scientific studies recently completed, and others just getting underway, the jury is not yet in on hoarding's definitive causes. Many theories exist. From observing behaviors of many object hoarders, there is a thought that they may share a genetic component with a first-order relative (mother, father, brother, sister) about 50% of the time.

There are social and anthropological theories connecting hoarding to a need for personal power, security, or having one's identity bolstered by what is owned, (perhaps an especially common pitfall here in the West). Its opposite, the scarcity theory, has been pretty well disproven by researchers. Hoarding does not seem related to having survived eras of great scarcity, such as the Great Depression. My own parents were in this age cohort and while I'd characterize their values and behaviors as thrifty, as was true of many of their friends, I don't see hoarding as a disorder any more common with this group than other groups.

Hoarding has been compared to PTSD or OCD, but thus far hoarding is not completely explained by either of them. It is interesting that object hoarders are less likely to endorse statements on surveys that feature a sense of support or acceptance by their families while growing up, as compared to either of the other two groups (OCD, PTSD). In one study, when asked what was going on at the time their hoarding developed, more than half responded with a memory of some important traumatic family event, most often associated with a loss or a death. Writers have surmised that their tenuous and insecure attachments to figures within their families combines with significant trauma, which in turn leads to a deep vulnerability to life circumstances and the corresponding need to soothe emotional pain with some illusion of control. We know some children face significant trauma essentially alone, and that in general, children often gravitate toward favorite objects and pets. Therefore, it's plausible that things or animals could be a second-best alternative to replace feelings of fear with safety, and to repair a sense of lost security. But much more research needs to be done. The same combination of impoverished beginnings and later trauma is found in many populations, those with addiction, depression, anxiety disorders, etc. Why does hoarding develop? That question has not been fully answered.

I would add that in my own experience, the tie with excessive unhealed trauma has been particularly striking in the hoarders I've interviewed. And, the research seems to support these impressions. Put side by side with the general population, one study found hoarders register six compared to three types of trauma experienced and 14 compared to 5 total episodes of trauma experienced in a lifetime.

It could be, (as I wrote in an article in April, 2011 issue of Counseling Today, "To Have and To Hold") that with a significantly greater amount of traumatic loss happening in a group of folks who already have special undetected vulnerabilities (insecure or disorganized attachment styles), something goes wrong in the brain's mechanisms for processing grief.

In the context of such hidden vulnerability, the next loss happens before the brain can fully recover from the last one, which sets into motion the urgent need for relief. We may be looking at a disorder that could be one possible sequel of abnormal grief, one so severe that it turns the corner into a particular compulsive behavior—an aggressive relief seeking through acquiring, holding onto, and resisting letting go of things or animals. What got me thinking in this direction was how one of my favorite hoarders described her predicament after the loss of her two husbands in quick succession; she unexpectedly found her second husband dead one day. She told me, "Thirteen pairs of pajamas make no sense, except to a hoarder. I guess when you think you've lost everything, you think at least you have your stuff." Her statement did make sense, and something clicked into place when she said it. An adult has attachment problems that have made her vulnerable since childhood. She then goes through a traumatic loss or series of losses. Her overwhelmed brain, broken down in its ability to process loss, reverts to a more rigid and chaotic pattern. She locks onto what can offer a more instant and uncomplicated form of relief without risking the disappointment and complexity humans bring to the situation, the risks that accompany all interpersonal relationships—something that can be controlled and always kept close such as objects or animals.

That the level of decompensation can be quite profound should not surprise us. People can devolve as well as evolve. The homeless will do bizarre things to survive, prisoners will learn to adapt to the worst extremes of degradation, and other of society's cast-offs or disadvantaged will work out shocking rituals that, while not part of what we think of as humanity, nonetheless keep them alive or give some comfort. *Apocalypse Now*, the hit movie that was a modern take off of Joseph Conrad's famous novel, *Heart of Darkness*, depicted a renegade officer in Vietnam who devolved into a caveman-warlord persona. There are accounts of small companies that in their insulation from the mainstream became a "Lord of the Flies" situation, metaphorically speaking. If something as complex as an organization can devolve, why not a single human being?

All this said, speculation is easy and cheap. Scientifically rigorous research is hard and expensive. It may be years until we know more for sure.

A Stage 5 Hoarder's Home

Cats, cats, and more cats

III. Get Ready for Hoarder Thinking and Feeling

Based on the previous chapters, we want to see hoarders as people who have resorted to extremes to get some means of comfort for an intense inner pain. These extreme behaviors are matched by extremes in thinking and feeling.

The regulation of affect (our feelings) is, in part, a socially mediated function. From birth we use attunement with another to manage affect and bring it into a tolerable range. Anyone who has ever seen a mom comfort a baby has witnessed this being done. A baby looks up into the caring face and feels on a bodily level that things will be all right and regains emotional control. We learn this with another and then become able to do it for ourselves. What is called the self-state can shift flexibly between contexts and we update ourselves, reassure ourselves, see the big picture, and continue to seek support when we need it from others.

Trauma disrupts these early abilities, and if a person self-isolates, their ability to manage affect deteriorates even further. Affect becomes more unpredictable and less controlled. Hoarders have very thin skin, are sometimes quick-tempered, moody, and may take a long time to get calm after something upsetting occurs. They are particularly avoidant of anxiety or stress and work out many ways to defer facing unpleasant tasks or realities. But the more they avoid, the more vulnerable they are to stress. Avoidance is reinforced because it works. They do get away, momentarily. Unfortunately, the price they pay is that avoidance only makes things scarier, or harder to deal with next time.

Dr. Randy Frost and his associates have studied how the hoarder's thinking changes, too. Much of what appears below is from his books, which appear under Sources. There is no one "typical" hoarder presentation. But what follows are some of the possibilities.

1. Hoarders may see objects or (eventually) animals as extensions of themselves. There is an object-identity fusion going on that is quite remarkable. An empty container of yogurt is

no longer just that, but it somehow says something about the hoarder.

2. There is an overblown sentimentality that gets extended to all sorts of things that start to serve as a tangible record of their lives. Parting with an object may feel like losing a limb, or disposing of mementoes or hand-me-downs may feel to the hoarder like throwing away part of someone else's life for good.

3. There are sometimes unusual beliefs about usefulness, waste, and responsibility. A hoarder may see the disposal of a few crumbs leftover in a container as a horrible display of waste. Or, they may save items such as toilet paper rolls or plastic bags from the store for someone (not even a specific someone) who may need it someday. If they can imagine such a use they tend to feel automatically responsible for carrying it out. Their wanting to become "shoulds" and then become musts. There seems to be no separation between idea and obligation.

4. There are problems with attention and distractibility. To hoarders, every stimuli has equal value and importance, so they can't filter, making it hard to focus anywhere.

5. There is also the opposite, a tendency to "lock on" to objects or ideas about objects. In the acquiring phase, hoarders may only need to touch an object to find they can't stop thinking about it. They may be persuaded to throw something away, but then dwell on it and hours later finally go retrieve it from the trash can or dumpster.

6. There are problems with categorization. Where most people would create one area for bills or reading materials, supplies or valuables, and group like items into those major categories, hoarders will create mini-categories for numerous items, which give rise to the stacks of stuff and those piles. They will treat each object as if it needs its own special due. Interestingly, in some hoarders this feature is contained to their own

possessions. It's at home where they get too emotionally involved with the item, but they can control this tendency in their workplace or when travel puts them around the objects of others.

7. This goes hand in hand then, with significant problems with memory. Hoarders tend use spatial location as a reminder system, taking a mental snapshot that they then have to keep updating as more and more things pile up. This, of course, breaks down at some point, as no one's memory can do it. But it is the reason why visitors cannot touch or move their things, as it disrupts their system. Ironically, hoarders often lose track of their most important possessions, and cleanup crews routinely find titles to houses, marriage licenses, mom's jewelry, and dad's war medals buried amidst piles of worthless trash.

8. There is extreme ambivalence for fear of not being perfect enough. This makes for tremendous difficulty in making decisions.

We all experience some ambivalence, but hoarders can stand in the middle of a room and spend most of the morning deciding where to put a piece of Tupperware. They live in extraordinary fear of making the wrong decision, and become agitated or shut down if others try to rush them.

9. There is a feature called elaborative processing. Hoarders are often highly creative people, but their creativity has run amok. They may look at the most commonplace objects, say bottle caps or the plastic rings from beverage seals, and imagine a whole new art form. They may go out and collect vast stores of "supplies" for a new project or hobby but then never follow through. The supplies remain with them for that imagined time when they will finally get around to it. This lack of follow through is a key complicating factor. Hoarders make regular runs to their favorite dollar stores or bargain basements, only to have clothes, supplies,

electronics, or whatever, go unused, often never even taken out of the original packaging.

10. There's a mental error called reification. This is mistaking an abstract idea or concept for a physical or concrete reality. I often give the example of the statue of Andrew Jackson in New Orleans. Jackson, the hero of the Battle of New Orleans, is admired for his backwoods know-how, military savvy, and indomitable spirit of American freedom. But if the City of New Orleans required everyone to take a rubbing of that statue and keep it on their person at all times so to incorporate those traits and preserve them, well, the good people of New Orleans would think it odd, to say the least. Not a hoarder, though. Hoarders look at objects in almost magical ways; they think of them as capable of preserving the essence of experiences, capable of human traits, like protection, or other special abilities. They feel a close identification, as if

it is the self they once had, or person they want to be.

11. I've mentioned the negative reinforcement that happens with avoidance above. There is of course the positive reinforcement, the "high" some hoarders get while getting new stuff. Just like a drug, the act of acquiring either calms them down or jazzes them up, depending on their emotional context and immediate needs. They will often admit doing the buying, getting, holding, stealing, or planning to use the item in an altered state. What's missing is the long view, the consequences of bringing the stuff or the animal back to a home already packed with things or other animals.

These features by no means exhaust all the twists and turns a hoarder's mind can take. Compulsive hoarders do not see any grey areas. They do not feel in a balanced way. This is not to say they can't recover their balance, but we must recognize we will often meet them with their defenses up and their extreme distortions well developed over time. The question is, can you work with and around these realities? Can you hold to your own reality and balance your reactions around a person who sometimes is quite literally perched on a pile of trash, who puts bottle caps ahead of people, or who doesn't see the danger posed by living with 50 cats and their excrement? It's not easy, but whoever said life was "supposed" to be easy, anyway?

IV. Talking to Hoarders: Connection, Uplift, and Developing Discrepancy

As a Rapid Resolution Therapist, I am trained in what I consider the cutting edge method of engaging troubled people. Dr. Jon Connelly, the method's creator, repeatedly tells us that, "Connection is a magnet you can use to affect the participant's energy level, mood, outlook, and behavior." Properly done, that's really the key. Next time you are in a restaurant or cafe, look around and spot the tables where people seem really into their conversation. They are leaning in, demonstrating interest, kind of dancing together from one comment to the next, even mirroring (called pacing) each other's posture, rate of breathing and emotional responses. The waiter will likely feel like he's interrupting something important. They are in a zone with each other and it's almost as if the whole room dropped away. That is connection. It is created by:

- Demonstrating your interest in understanding the other person's experience

- Clarifying and demonstrating your understanding

- Being positive, interesting, appreciative, and incorporating appropriate humor

- Aligning with breathing and matching volume, speed of speech, and body position of the other person

Hoarders are usually not in a good place emotionally or open to much connection. They are often down on themselves and just waiting to get that attitude from someone else. You'll have to work a little more on your end than you would with most to get through, but get through you can.

We are trained in RRT to get our communications through three hoops. Hoop number one is to avoid disagreement. Hoop number two is to avoid being poisonous. Hoop number three is to make what we say understandable to the subconscious. We use effect-driven language to quickly get through these three hoops and establish connection with our clients.

Hoop number one is about stating the obvious, something that can't be refuted. A hoarder may be living in quite a mess, but on first meeting I'll often appreciatively notice something in their stash, some evidence of a pet interest. It may be plastic milk jugs, framed pictures, or a certain type of news journal or a certain type of cat. I'll use whatever is in the environment to break the ice and demonstrate interest in the hoarder.

With Chester, whom you'll hear about throughout this book, I first said, as his two giant Dobermans sniffed me,

"So you're a dog lover. Take me in and show me *their* house."

I was stating what was situationally true, with a friendly irony that Chester appreciated. It met no disagreement from him. He laughed, admitting that his dogs were number one and had "people privileges."

The second hoop is to avoid any language that fuses the hoarder's identity with problematic traits or behaviors. It is a delicate balance to demonstrate understanding of the trouble the person is in without making the trouble about them, i.e., without making them the repository of the trouble.

Hoop number three is to aim what you want heard at the subconscious. This can be done in various ways, through subtle repetition, through voice inflection, which emphasizes some words over others, through putting problematic behavior in the past, or through separation and protection of identity. There is also a tool we use called the wedge, where you separate an erroneous belief from being taken as truth.

For example, a hoarder might say,

"I'm never organized. I spend hours and hours trying to straighten up this room, but don't seem to get very far."

My ear picks up, first, the all or nothing thinking; secondly, how closely they've aligned problematic behavior with identity; and third, how they kind of predict their own future (devoid of different outcomes) from a painful past. It's as if she just introduced herself, "Hello there, my name is Disorganization. I've squandered the best years of my life in fruitless effort, and it's never going to be any different."

I might respond, "There's been a concern about less organization than you'd like. And you're looking to straighten things up, now that you've come this far."

It is very subtle, but in my statement, I'm already trying to move around dysfunctional thinking and establish connection. I do it with what is called the **invisible tense change**, (There's been), already putting the problematic pattern her mind is causing in the past. It's also putting the pattern outside her, one step removed, as it were. This will make it easier for me to frame the pattern as something her mind has been doing, and recruit her to see it that way, too, rather than a fundamental aspect of her identity. If it's just something the mind has been doing, then that gives us all sorts of leverage, because it's adjustable. The contraction "There's" flashes by her without her even noticing it, but starts to accomplish this. I minimize the failed attempts and unproductive hours spent by not mentioning them at all.

You may have noticed I did not phrase it, "You've been concerned about having less organization, or, "**being** less organized..." which may sound more syntactically correct to the ear. Why? Because words like "having" and "being" connote possession of the undesired trait, putting it closer to her identity when I want to protect her identity and keep it separate. People have colds. I don't want her having disorganization to be akin to a chronic disease. And I sure don't want it superimposed on her identity.

I might even pause after the word "to" and after the word "now" for just an instant, which has the effect of grouping the words, "straighten things up now...." This is called a **dressed command**. Without my saying so out loud, she hears on a deep level there's hope of change. And she may feel a strange, new urge to get at it.

The last thing going on in this example is ending with the positive. Notice how I mention the negative factor first and the positive last. You can't always tell how a person's mind is going to organize auditory input, but I'm trying to stack the deck in my favor. Most people put a mental comma in the middle of a two-part statement like mine, particularly if there is any pause. Ending with the positive saves the best for last. This has the effect of putting the brakes on the first part, the negative, and shifting into forward gear on the last part, the positive.

Visually, the statement might be heard like this, where the lighter text represent a stoppage of the negative influence and the bold letters represent what the ear hears last, and therefore pays more attention to: There's been a concern about less organization than you'd like. **And you're looking to straighten things up, now that you've come this far.**

To say it another way, the ear leans away from the trouble end of the seesaw (minimizing it) and leans into the positive end, the hope and possibility in the situation. The subconscious just heard on a very deep level that there can be a swing or momentum from one state to the other, rather than assuming one ends up stuck in the negative until the end of time.

I also capture her inner strength in staying with it despite discouraging outcomes. Without explicitly saying it, I am celebrating her muscle, her backbone, her gumption, her intention to be out of the painful present and into a healthier situation, by rewarding any progress she achieved on her own. No matter how little, it's worth mentioning. Folks down on themselves routinely screen out their own everyday achievements.

This all creates what we call "uplift." I've avoided paraphrasing or parroting the poisonous things she has said to herself or others have said repeatedly, and I've just spoken a word of hope to the subconscious. That part of her mind gets it— that I see her in a positive light and am already engaged with her in creating a brighter future.

This is not just sprinkling sunshine or the power of positive thinking. The language changes are far more technical than that and take time to master. My statement can't be so far ahead of her perceived ability that it's unreal. Notice the effect on the hoarder if after her opening line I come back with,

"You've done a great job here, and day by day I'm sure you can get your whole house in order."

Her brain registers the dissonance between what is said and what she really believes. What I said gets coded, "Not true," and I fail to get through Hoop No. 1. How do I know enough to say I'm sure she can do it? She's standing in the middle of evidence to the contrary and her failures are the only thing she has been focused on. She sees through my comment as a piece of shallow, false reassurance.

Now notice the effect if I respond as most therapists would, zeroing in on the pain with so-called empathy:

"I hear that you are not very organized, and you're very troubled by all the effort that has not worked out for you."

The subconscious mind hears the fusion of identity (you) with "not organized." It also hears a magnification of all the trouble in her life with the addition of "very." That's the way awareness works. We magnify that which we focus on. The typical mental health worker is trained to show great respect for feelings and is sold on the idea that people need to "get their feelings out" to heal. He or she will linger on the pain, thinking they are joining with the client and taking a step toward that all-important disgorgement.

In fact, what happens for the client is they feel worse, more hopeless, more screwed up. The unconscious thinks, "Wow, I must be really bad, my troubled state of mind is the first thing this expert noticed."

Also, we need to bear in mind the stigma and connotations that still exist in the public about mental health and mental health terminology. The words "very troubled" may be how the psychiatrist chose to describe Aunt Millie's psychotic break to the family 50 years ago as they were committing her to the insane asylum.

To continue, the subconscious hears, "effort has not worked," closely followed by "you," which can sound like an indictment (Effort has not worked, you!) to a shame-based person. This will unwittingly embed more blame and shame and disrupt the connection.

To sum up, we've been looking at using effect-driven language to build uplift and connection. If you train yourself to think about your words having a forward-looking, uplifting effect, and you simultaneously protect identity from illness language, you are most of the way there. If you then say them in your mind first, putting yourself in the shoes of the hoarder, you will get better and better at dismissing what won't have a good effect and at keeping what will, thereby creating the connection you want.

Developing Discrepancy is a tool that comes from Motivational Interviewing. It relies on asking open-ended questions about the painful present and subtly, gently starting to juxtapose them with a hoped-for future. This is crucial with someone who is as deeply ambivalent about change as a hoarder. To do this effectively you have to spend some time finding out what is most important to the person.

Nobody ever changes, motivational interviewing believes, because they were confronted, exhorted, lectured, or reminded of the fearful consequences that await inaction. They don't change because they have "hit bottom," suffered enough, or absorbed enough guilt about their impact on others. Even outright punishment doesn't seem powerful enough to turn people around, as evidenced by our growing prison systems and rate of repeat offenses. These methods fail miserably to motivate real change over the long run.

What does seem to work is when a person **identifies something important to them, a cherished value or vision of themselves** that, when stood up alongside the painful present, begs the question, "What do I need to do to get myself from here to there?" If the helper can get himself or herself out of the line of sight of that question, and not become part of the problem, someone to be resisted, you have the makings of a powerful collaborative relationship.

The helper comes alongside, looking at advantages and disadvantages both of the status quo and the desired change, which begins to develop the discrepancy. The helper carefully (maybe a little at this visit, maybe more two or three visits from now) asks questions about what is important, guiding the hoarder gently into articulating their own goals, and listening for readiness to look at what it would take to get from here to there. Again, this is not something learned easily or overnight. But a taste of it and what can be done comes in the following excerpt from the book *Digging Out*, by Tompkins and Hartl, found in Sources at the end (permission obtained for use of excerpt from Copyright Clearance Center).

Ted, the son, has been gently teasing out a discussion of the advantages and disadvantages of his mother, Laura, accepting some help for her hoarding problem. He gets her permission to have the conversation in the first place, and then her cooperation in brainstorming a list of both advantages and disadvantages. At this point they have thoroughly gone over both lists and he has checked for agreement and completeness at each step. Then he picks up on her own goal, her vision of a better future:

Laura: Well, I guess if I let you and your sister help me, I'd get to see you two more often. I know it's hard on you to see my house, but I do miss you.

Ted: Yes, we'd like to see you more often too, Mom. That would be a big advantage for me, too. What else?

Laura: I can't think of anything else.

Ted: I have an idea Want to hear it?

Laura: Sure

Ted: Well, if we could straighten things a little better, we might be able to have Jamie's birthday here, like the old days. We used to have terrific birthday parties here, remember?

Laura: Yes, I remember. I miss those, too. That would be wonderful. Do you really think we could do that?

Ted: Well, I don't see why not. We'd just have to focus on a couple of places in the house, maybe the living room and the kitchen. We might be able to do that? What do you think?

Laura: That would be great.

This is not trickery, but the fruits of patient listening, true collaboration, and letting the goal emerge. She owns the pros and cons of moving forward and he examines them with her, without sugarcoating or exaggeration. His ear catches her wish to see family more and he extends her goal to include more contact with the granddaughter. He then connects the real possibility of getting to that goal with steps needed to get out of the painful present. He asks permission to share his thought. It's not about being pushy, pedantic, authoritarian, or demanding, all of which frighten and enrage hoarders. Frightening because they feel pressured. Enraged because they've heard it all before and resent anyone's taking their freedom of choice from them. This exchange works because Ted is able to stand alongside his mom as a collaborator, and he avoids any flare-ups or battle of wills and just lets the discrepancy do its work.

I've been with many drug addicts and alcoholics as they get into their recovery and have asked them why they finally became sober. It's not the gems of wisdom others shared in group or the enlightened and sometimes frightening drug education counselors gave them, valuable though these all may be. It's not the severity of consequences, either. Indeed, many lost everything, only to go out and use again. It's usually a statement like, "I think I finally realized, if I kept going like this, I'd never see my kid again." Something finally emerged that, when stood up against the painful present, clearly illuminated the gap between here and there, and the person decided "here" wasn't so attractive after all, and that "there" is where they really wanted to be.

I realize these skills are not familiar to all readers or necessarily in everyone's comfort zone. They weren't in mine. For years I had talked to clients from an "I'm the well counselor" and "You're the poor sick client" perspective. It's not that I'm cruel or more arrogant than most. My graduate education, combined with being immersed in a medical model for years, instilled poisonous language in me, which I used without a second thought. With considerable effort, I have been trained to quit doing it and do something else now. I would not expect most therapists, let alone family members, to have an extensive background in the approach I am advocating here. But I am featuring it because I believe language and connection are among the most powerful natural tools we as human beings can use. You do not need a Ph.D. to lean into this approach and begin experimenting with it. Even one shift in your responses, for example, you omit the hoarder's descriptions of past failures and instead flow into casual enunciations of what's already progressing, what's valuable to the hoarder, and your belief they are already on their way there will have a tremendous impact.

It's not necessary that they see the destination (what we call the model) clearly, only that they *see* that you see it. For if, as Dr. Jon Connolly taught me, they conceive of **you** envisioning a model of a better life for them, then they can't help but conceive of it, at some level, in their own mind, too. It will surprise you when they tell someone else they look forward to your visits, that you have already helped them a great deal, even though you can't really put your finger on how. Believe me, the help is real and it can be done by anyone willing to pay a little attention to what they say and how they say it.

Past this point, I will assume you have gained some trust and rapport and are moving toward some kind of contract with a hoarder, some kind of agreement that will guide whatever they want to get done about their habitat. From now on, the communications alternate between offering connection and ideas that provide the scaffolding of change (addressed in the Follow Up section), sprinkled liberally with praise—honest praise for any show of courage or actual effort, no matter how small.

Always Fall Back on Connection and Discrepancy

Hoarders frequently balk or bog down in worry about many things that seem tangential or out of their control. They are sensitive to any development that would move them out of their comfort zone. What usually works, once you've got an agreement on the goal, is to gently review that goal at such moments. And, by the way, this is one reason why it is important to have the goal written down as part of an overall plan. That way it doesn't appear you are pulling out a trump card from the bottom of the deck, but merely appealing to a benchmark that all parties previously agreed to.

One gentleman I worked with was moving along nicely, clearing rooms in his overstuffed house one by one, but then came close to bogging down about his vast collection of hand tools. Working with tools had been very close to his identity and given him much fulfillment. He wanted to hang onto most of them or wait to find the perfect handyman who would appreciate and take care of what he had to give. Getting it just right caused substantial anxiety and his whole project started to stall. We sat down and devoted an hour to revisiting his goals of becoming more social, getting his home to where he could invite new friends in, and reconnecting with his daughter and have her comfortably come for a visit. I didn't run roughshod over his anxiety or focus on the impasse. I dropped back to my skills of creating connection and uplift, and gradually re-introduced the centrality of his goals. There are many moments in helping hoarders like that, where the foundation you previous laid really pays off.

V: Have a Plan

Ok. You've been laying a foundation for weeks, maybe months, maybe even years. Your hoarder is into a solid state of connection with you and more easily talks about the benefits of making a change over the benefits of staying with the status quo or what Motivational Interviewing refers to as "Change Talk." Maybe there have been some mini-experiments, where you tested the waters working alongside the hoarder, tackling one small pile of stuff for an hour or two, or adopting out one recently acquired animal, just so they could see it could be done. Maybe they even began to sort or discard on their own and they proudly showed you their progress the next time you came by.

It is now that the hoarder needs a concrete plan and needs your support. They need it because of their problems with mental processing—namely their distractibility, their extreme ambivalence, their over-sentimentality, their coding of improvement as taking on impossible demands, and any or all of the psychological factors listed so far. Now is not the time to step back thinking the hoarder can take it from here, nor the time to do things ad hoc, because the hoarder has been thinking that way for years and will quickly get lost in details or get overwhelmed by the magnitude of what is about to take place in his or her life.

As mentioned above, the solidification of the hoarder's goals leads naturally into a contract. The contract is a master plan with the overall goal(s) and description of other parts of the plan clearly written out:

- which areas of the house or the overall situation will be addressed

- where items will be recycled, donated, sold, or dumped

- which resource people will be needed, such as cleaning crews, animal control experts, therapists, professional organizers, etc.

- which supplies will be needed, such as boxes, tape, trash bags

- where will the staging area be—where those involved in cleaning up can bring larger parcels of stuff and sort them into smaller containers for appropriate disposal or storage

- what is the timeline for each targeted area of activity

- what are the responsibilities of the various players

Everyone most directly involved should sign the contract. It should be reviewed with anyone who will be moving in and out of the situation playing even a limited role, for example, a trash hauling or hazardous waste disposal service who may only be on site for a matter of hours.

The plan assembles a team who will work with the hoarder to accomplish the goal. How many team members will be needed or how extensive the plan will depend on the stage of the hoard and the stage of dissipation of the hoarder. It's not uncommon for a team to include a professional organizer, therapist, nurse, a social worker from an involved agency, a representative from county public health, animal control or code personnel, a trusted friend or family member for support, even clergy or volunteers from a religious community. Any of these can play a crucial role in supporting or defining limits for the hoarder at just the right time. All of them together provide a powerful network of ideas and combined strength to meet a daunting situation.

Sometimes family can construct the plan, especially if there is one member who can remain objective and has skills in thinking through the steps. But many times family will be too emotional or too close to the situation to do this. I think social workers and counselors are uniquely trained to do what's called a psychosocial assessment, which takes an overview of a person and initiates plans to match resources to identified needs. A public health nurse or home health nurse may be able to do the same, depending on their experience. A professional organizer may have many of the logistical skills, but will need to work in tandem with a health care professional to cover the emergent physical and psychological needs of the hoarder. But whoever the plan maker is, it is important to include the hoarder. The plan should be constructed collaboratively. At every point you want their buy-in and the good ideas they have to contribute. It's their life, after all, that will finally be affected by the changes enacted.

There are two current approaches to making a plan, and I want to touch on them briefly because they each have merit in their respective contexts.

Harm Reduction

The first is called a Harm Reduction approach. It is useful when the hoarder is characterized by low insight, extreme levels of denial, or exaggerated resentment, mistrust, or hopelessness. Harm Reduction is a public health approach first conceived by Marlatt in 1998 to help minimize the risks of intravenous drug abuse rather than trying to force chronic addicts to stop using entirely.

This approach is well laid out and applied to hoarding in Tompkins and Hartl's *Digging Out*, found in the Sources section.

It involves several assumptions: (1) That those who intervene can do real harm. Some situations may be better left alone. So when in doubt, do no harm. (2) That it is not necessary to stop all hoarding, but rather that any step in the right direction is welcomed and can mean a valuable improvement. 3) That the hoarder is the essential member of the team and has the right to make choices. Clean up crews will usually give the hoarder control over which rooms to start on and what to throw out. As respected participants, hoarders can often come up with creative solutions no one else might have thought of. 4) It is assumed that change will be slow, with setbacks (what they call "contract failures") expected, which don't necessarily mean the overall plan has failed. Many times if anxiety is running high, or in the event of an outright melt down, a hoarder may just need a couple days' break to regroup, and then the plan can resume.

What I like about this approach is it takes things in small bites. Allow me to describe. With the team, the hoarder goes around his or her home and prioritizes targeted areas and living conditions that affect 1) safety and 2) health and comfort, in that order. For instance, a stove covered with paper or a blocked exit is actually a lot bigger deal than a toilet or sink that doesn't drain perfectly or a screen door hanging off its hinge. An infestation of rodents or insects or buildup of animal excrement is a bigger deal than a backyard filled with discarded appliances.

These kinds of threats to health or safety require immediate attention. A Harm Reduction approach not only assesses personal safety, but medical and psychological needs, as well as imminent financial risks. If a hoarder has tossed unopened mail on a pile for the last year, he may be unaware of notices of violations, overdrafts, unreceived payments of fines, impending evictions, etc. He may be unaware, therefore, of pending legal actions that could result in having to vacate his home or loss of the home altogether.

The team works together to prioritize danger areas and craft realistic goals for the hoarder. Goals are concrete and specific, reachable, given a specific time frame, and are worded so they can be monitored or measured in some way. Different team members may have different goals, and these are included on the master plan sheet, but positioned so as not to compete against each other.

The visiting nurse may want to see an organized pillbox and disposal of all expired medicines over the short haul. Over the long haul, she may ultimately want to see elevated blood sugars come down. A son or daughter may want to see threats to a parent's safety removed immediately, like fire hazards or likelihood of falling. They may ultimately favor selling the parental home rather than financing its repair. A landlord may want a more comprehensive correction up front, like a general cleanup and repair by a professional crew. Each factor in the living situation is fashioned as a harm reduction target, given a priority, and put in a hierarchy, in terms of immediacy and safety versus long-term and desired (which can be listed as two separate columns on the master plan).

Hoarders themselves are prone to lose sight of the big picture or, the opposite, overwhelm themselves with it. They do it by focusing on minutia or going for long-range goals without first covering intermediary steps. But by having a cooperatively constructed plan, you have the needed checks and balances. Everyone knows what will be worked on in what order and whoever's on site can re-orient the hoarder to the plan. Good plans are works in progress, so the whole planning team meets at regular intervals to tweak it and adjust for unforeseen circumstances.

General Clean Ups

The other approach to planning is geared to a general cleanup. While a harm reduction plan usually unfolds one target at a time over a longer period, a general cleanup is a time-limited project that is usually more intensive and comprehensive. It can take place over several days and aims to get required improvements in place before team members disperse. The hoarder, the family, or treatment team members may electively design these improvements. It can be used when the hoarder has significant insight and has elected to do a comprehensive job quickly. Or it can be used when things have come to a head, the hoarder's situation is on the radar of city or county authorities, and there is limited time to get the types of corrections and the extent of corrections that are mandated. Please note that with general cleanups we are talking about large scale changes that will take place quickly, so counselors need to prepare the hoarder beforehand, if possible, for how their changed environment is likely to affect them.

In the majority of these cases and, contrary to the fears of the hoarder, authorities want to work with the situation whenever possible. Animal control will withhold prosecution if an animal hoarder will surrender some of their animals and bring the home up to minimum standards for space, feeding, and safe care of a small number of domestic pets. Cities and county governments do not want to permanently separate residents from salvageable homes, because they do not want an inventory of vacant buildings on their hands. Code officials and inspectors will usually work with a hoarder who shows reasonable progress in doing necessary cleaning and repairs. But make no mistake about it; they all come into the situation with the authority to enforce. They may have already spoken to the district attorney and carry a warrant or a court order to enter and seize the premises, if need be.

Matt Paxton, a cleanup expert often featured on A&E's show *Hoarders*, has written a nice book, *The Secret Lives of Hoarders* in which he goes over the important aspects of a good cleanup effort. He elevates the importance of the team effort and mutual accountability for meeting goals. There is usually a morning meeting with all players on each day of a cleanup project. The hoarder is congratulated for getting through any tough spots and publicly praised for any individual effort. I like two of his ideas included in the book, the ideas of "Homework" and "The Fire List."

Homework is way of testing how much a hoarder can do on his or her own when the team is not around. After the day's work is done, the hoarder is given a small task to complete overnight, usually a small additional area or box of stuff to sort through and make discard/keep/recycle/donate decisions on their own. This tells something about their tolerance for stress when support is not available and the likelihood they will be able to follow through on tasks after the team has disbanded and they are on their own again.

The Fire List is an exercise where the hoarder makes a list of everything they would want to keep if there was a fire, and the list is limited to one side of a page of paper. They are then timed and given two minutes (the amount of time they would have to get out if their house ever caught on fire) to find and group their most important possessions they could carry out in one trip.

No one beats the clock. The two minutes is gone in a blink. This defeats their assumption, often repeated to others, that they know where everything is. It makes them question if they could actually preserve their treasures under their current cluttered circumstances. This puts into new perspective the need for ongoing order and a decision-making process about bringing new stuff home. Ideally, they begin to muster some organizational skills and start being more selective in their approach to shopping or acquiring.

An additional benefit is that the team can assist as the cleanup progresses, and be on the lookout for any unfound items on the list. The list is copied and tacked up in each room, so each team member can help find the things the Hoarder says are indispensable. When those items are uncovered, there's a shared feeling of success. This builds a bond of trust as the hoarder realizes no one is out to deceive him and that can make the rest of the cleanup go more smoothly.

A top to bottom professional cleanup is a complex logistical affair. Professional organizers, seasoned cleanup teams, or moving specialists are often in a great position to orchestrate the actual steps. But all whose writings I've studied, or websites I've visited, emphasize the cleanup has to be matched to the hoarder's true motivation and tolerance for stress. If they run into frank denial or repeated cancellations or delays, they know a cleanup would be fruitless; the home would just be filled up again in a year or less.

Ambushes by family (blitzkrieg cleanups), secret clean ups, ultimatums, all forms of forced cleanup, are the worst experiences for all concerned. For one, they don't usually work. And second, the stress they cause is hardly worth the outcome.

One hoarder I worked with, Chester, was interviewed with me on public radio. He told of his ex-wife and daughter descending on his house one weekend. He was mortified that his neighbors were learning of the extent of his hoard, as his ex and daughter hauled trash bag after trash bag out to the curb until they formed a solid wall about six feet high along the whole frontage of his property. He was furious to find out they threw away some of his most prize memorabilia from his trips to Latin America. When they returned about two years later to check on him, the house was back to the way it was, if not worse. "Why?" they asked, exasperated. He sat stonily on the couch petting his dog in his lap, and gave no answer. "Well, they declared, it would be the last d***ed time they would ever come to help!" He accurately said between clenched teeth, "I never asked for your help!"

This kind of reaction can spoil a hoarder's response to any help for years to come or even for the rest of his life. Forced clean outs not only produce severe resistance, they are traumatizing and can bring on a health calamity such as a stroke or a mental breakdown. The rule, First, do no harm, is a good one.

Under the Gun

That being said, there are times when hoarders are under the gun to produce some improvement in the habitat, and animal control or code inspectors have to go forward before their motivations are in place or they can even be adequately prepared. These are usually in the context of an ordinance violation, the forcing of the issue by neighbors or landlord, or when some sort of imminent danger exists, either to people or animals. It usually involves a stage 4 or 5 hoarder, and even if the hoarder complies and gets the home to the point where it can be safely entered, it does not insure it won't ultimately be condemned and they will lose it anyway.

When animal control authorities have to remove even one sick or dying animal, they've just taken jurisdiction of the case and become enforcers of laws against animal cruelty; they have to act to protect the welfare of any remaining animals. Euthanasia is not a uniform option, but with some animals, it's the only one that makes sense. This confronts an animal hoarder with his or her worst nightmare: that someone will come and take their beloved pets and even put them to death. They just don't see the suffering their own neglect has inflicted and how euthanasia is a decent option to more suffering in situations where emergency veterinary medicine can't make a difference. All they know is that they are losing a beloved friend, one even like a child to them, and will now face devastating loneliness once more.

The first case I ever volunteered on, mentioned at the start of the book, took me to the home of a wife, husband, and their adult son all living together with 77 cats. It was August in Florida. As I arrived,

I was given a re-breather mask, but before I could get it on, the front door opened and the smell from inside made me momentarily double over, coughing and gagging, until I could get my breath. My eyes were stinging. The husband came out first and we all saw the open diabetic sores on his swollen, overweight legs. Living in conditions that could only be described as abject squalor, he immediately rose to the top as our most pressing concern. Their home had long since lost air conditioning. He was pale, pasty, and looked so ill that he could topple over at any minute. But he was still standing with the use of his cane and ready to run interference for his wife. Despite all his excuses for her, we learned she had over two years taken in every field stray and abandoned neighborhood cat she could, refusing to spay or neuter any of them.

She kept most of them cramped in small cages, but many ran free, urinating and defecating on every surface, high and low. Many were injured from fighting in close quarters for scarce food and space. She was unaware one was dead in the dryer and another looked like it had starved to death behind a bed. We later learned the wiring behind most of the walls was ruined because they had urinated right into the plug outlets. The urine had followed the wires, running down behind walls, and with the water from unfixed leaks in the roof, the walls had grown a coat of black mold, so that the air hung with a thick, dank smell, no matter where you turned.

The family had jury-rigged a web of extension cords from the outlets that were still functional, giving themselves power to back rooms from the kitchen. The fire marshal who reported to the scene right after me took one look at this and immediately went white in the face, too. He took out his clipboard and starting writing. Code personnel shook their heads in amazement. The family had somehow dug out a portion of tile floor and beneath, through the concrete pad of the house under their lanai, (as the patio room is called in Florida homes), to make a giant litter box about eight feet long, five feet wide, and three feet deep. It was more than full. To tell you the truth, until I looked closely at its contents, I didn't recognize it as a litter box at first. I thought it was a fresh grave.

In conditions like these, priorities shift rapidly from merely supporting the hoarder in self-chosen change, to enacting interventions to remedy what could amount to a life-threatening situation. It is understood the hoarder isn't going to be calling the shots or given much time to prepare. Everyone in this family needed an immediate medical check. They had been breathing in levels of ammonia unsafe for humans, and living in proximity to possible zoonotic disease carriers for a long time. Zoonotic diseases are a class of very potent and potentially lethal diseases that can be passed from animals to humans, by virus or bacteria, which accompany the presence of excessive animal populations and their droppings. Human fecal matter and other biohazardous waste (blood, urine, used needles) can be equally dangerous. Rodents, flies, and other insects can ingest various toxins and quickly pass them all throughout a house through saliva and excrement. The Black Death that wiped out much of Europe in the Middle Ages came from the hanta virus, commonly found in rodent excrement.

If you go into a home in which any of these dangers are present, please protect yourself. Don't worry about the hoarder's feelings. Wear protective gear. I mentioned a re-breather mask. You may also need a Tyvek suit, shoe covers, latex gloves, and protective eyewear. I realize you may not have these hanging in your closet at home, so ask your local Animal Services, local Fire Department or Police Department if you can borrow equipment, or they can tell you where you can purchase it. Many drug stores have latex gloves and basic facemasks that can get you by in less severe situations. I don't usually touch a hoarder's things, unless I am demonstrating how to sort and discard. But anytime I need to touch an item or a surface, I use gloves and hand sanitizer afterward. And if there is even a hint of particulates in the air, I use a mask.

But I digress. In the intervention I've been describing, the wife had long since run out of her anti-depressant medicine, which she got through the public health clinic and she'd gone for weeks without while her depression worsened, with added delusions and periodic hallucinations. She needed to see a psychiatrist at once. The son was in his late twenties, also depressed and untreated. We learned that he had been making suicidal threats to his parents over the last year. If he had been under 18, Child Protective Services would have been immediately called and a report filed. The husband was in such extremity, that had he not complied with the plan to get him immediately in for medical evaluation, we would have called in Adult Protective Services.

Animal Control set up a staging area in the front yard where they sorted the sickest animals from the ones that just needed nutrition, hydration, or minor wound care. None of this was pleasing to the hoarder and her family was on edge as she became edgier by the moment. I could see where it was going and made the decision to have them all join me at a nearby Panera Bread, where I offered to buy them coffee and just "take a break" for a while. Luckily, they accepted.

I listened to the wife's story of unremitting grief over the past 15 years, starting with the death of her mother, the loss of jobs, her husband's loss of health, a hurricane that wrecked the roof without promised government funds to repair it, the indignities suffered by having to go on welfare, and perceived poor treatment by the medical system. Her cats had been her solace in this sea of downward mobility and grief. As I connected, I began to broker the news that they could not return to their own home until code enforcement and Animal Control cleared it for re-habitation. I encouraged them to take it day-by-day, hour-by-hour, if need be. It was crisis counseling pure and simple.

That homecoming never took place. The home was deemed a total loss, and even before it could be scheduled to be bulldozed, caught fire one night. The faulty wiring sparked and caught in a bedroom packed to the ceiling with clothes, furniture, and bedding she had inherited when her mother died. It was so packed with stuff the firemen could not get in through any window or force any door inward. It burned to the ground within fifteen minutes. In three short days this family lost all their possessions, all their pets, their home, their shelter. They were put up in temporary housing and became totally dependent on the state for all their needs. They eventually moved back to West Virginia, where she had been born.

A forced cleanup is always a measure of the last resort. These are the situations most commonly portrayed on TV, and the public may have gotten the idea that's the only way to do it. However, they are the least desired by those who do this work all the time. There is no going back once the wheels are set in motion and authorities begin to execute their sworn duties. Frequent family meetings and consultations with the response team are still essential. They can clarify the process and mitigate some of the stress, similar to when support teams brief families during natural disasters. But make no mistake, there is still major league stress on everyone, and a fragile hoarder is at the center of it all.

There should, if at all possible, be a mental health professional assigned daily to monitor the hoarder's mental state, and if physically frail, a nurse or physician available who can provide a wellness check, evaluate any conditions, coordinate medications, or get the hoarder to a hospital or clinic if treatment is needed.

This next part is important. If the hoarder or any family members are thought to be dangerous or to possess firearms, or if there is any evidence of on-site drug activity, current intoxication, or domestic violence, I personally would not respond until law enforcement has arrived. I would wait until such weapons are secured or irate family members are brought under control. Hoarders are not generally violent people, but you don't want to be the first one at the home and push your luck against anyone of questionable mental status or judgment. As the situation heats up and a hoarder and their family is learning they may be forced from their home, or being separated from their animals, things can get nasty. In our county we have a Task Force and when severe hoarding situations are reported, efforts are coordinated through United Way. They contact appropriate agencies and task force members and make all attempts to get needed personnel on scene before the intervention begins. If it's severe, the police are always there first, because you just never know what you are walking into.

The author (left) joins the Operations Director of Animal Control in responding to a call

VI. Navigating the Waters

River pilots, when they enter a tricky or
unfamiliar part of a river, do two things: they take
more frequent readings with their instruments, and
they rely on their crew, who can be their eyes and
ears from multiple points around the ship. The
amount of communication goes up, not down.

This is a useful principle to remember whether
as a first responder you are new to this population,
or as a family member, you have never gotten this
involved before. No two hoarding situations are
identical. Every hoarder has his or her own unique
mix of cognitive and emotional vulnerabilities that
can change the climate of helping from one visit to
the next. As a general rule, when things heat up, I
increase my visits and stay in closer touch with
other team members to check on the hoarder's
status, the status of the plan, and to check for
accuracy of understandings among team members.

One team member may have unexpectedly
been privy to a piece of data that the whole team
needs or done a significant intervention, within their

own role, that moves the plan along or necessitates a midcourse correction. Another side of this is that the hoarder's emotional reactivity, memory problems, and cognitive distortions often get the best of them under stress. They can inadvertently jam up communications by telling different people different things at different times. The team needs to stay in touch with itself during times of increased stress, to make sure everyone really is on the same page.

Mental Health Services

Regardless of what angle you enter a hoarding situation from, or whatever your role, everyone on the team needs to be aware the hoarder's emotional and psychological issues can take center stage at any moment in the process. In all situations where the hoarder lacks good insight, good motivation, adequate confidence to move forward, and adequate capacity to tolerate stress, it is probably best to have a mental health professional visiting on at least a weekly basis and working with the hoarder to navigate the waters.

What exactly does the mental health provider do and what training do they need to have? At a minimum, they need to have graduated from an accredited graduate level counseling or psychology program and become licensed to practice within the state they are delivering service. They will typically have a Master's degree, a Ph.D., or a Psy.D. as their terminal degree and will be licensed as a social worker (LCSW), a mental health counselor (LMHC or LPC), a marriage and family counselor (LMFT), a psychologist (Ph.D.), a nurse practitioner (ARNP) or psychiatrist (MD).

If working for the government or a private company, they must have authorization through their agency to deliver services in a home setting and have actively met their continuing education requirement and maintained their malpractice insurance. Their license must be active and up to date, free of revocations at any time, and free of current suspensions, ethical violations, or other disciplinary actions.

Many states offer directories within the state's main healthcare or licensing website where you can search provider names, look up records and verify their credentials and status of good standing in meeting these requirements. You can also see if they've ever had any complaints filed against them.

A mental health provider is capable of performing a comprehensive assessment, constructing an intelligent treatment plan, coordinating resources, and collaborating with others, such as primary physicians or psychiatrists. They should have foundational skills in listening and interacting supportively with clients and families to form a working relationship, awareness of boundaries and ethical issues, aware of cultural issues that may be at play, and an array of interventions that they've learned to enact the treatment plan. They should be able to manage emergency mental health conditions, such as how to assess for suicidality and know how to get a client into a higher level of care, when needed.

Beyond this, obviously it would be good they show evidence of having worked with hoarders. But unfortunately, this is something that is still a rarity. Keep in mind some clinicians, working for agencies that routinely go into homes, such as Hospice, Family Preservation programs, or those working with Home Health Agencies or the Health Department may have encountered hoarding before and amassed some practical experience. It is even better if they've done reading or research on their own, and best of all if they are members of a Task Force in their area, as they may have become an identified resource and picked up opportunities for involvement. Don't be afraid to ask them to describe what sources or experiences have shaped the way they understand hoarding.

I recommend only using a provider who has gone out to a hoarder's home and conducted sessions with them on site. This is not the kind of disorder that you can understand by only meeting with a client in a comfortable office. Practically speaking, you need to see the hoard to assign it a Stage (1-5); and interventions are best done in the home, where the hoarder is most likely to be triggered. Providers also need to see the home from time to time to check on progress. One hoarder I know confessed he'd been going to the VA for 15 years to be treated for depression and anxiety, working with many of the same staff over that time, but none of them was aware of his home situation. Hoarders will not fully disclose what they are doing when they don't have to. Unfortunately, most providers working out of offices won't think to include this in their initial assessment.

Treatment

Much of the literature on intervention with hoarding to date has been written by clinicians from primarily a cognitive behavioral orientation. This is the therapy developed first by Albert Ellis, Ph.D., that focuses on unmasking the erroneous and upsetting aspects of irrational thoughts people might entertain. Through the years it has been combined with behavioral perspectives and techniques to include exercises that use a person's action system to engage in interesting experiments that can change those irrational beliefs.

A CBT therapist would be interested in getting the client to evaluate troubling thoughts that drive distressing feelings and actions or doing behavioral interventions that then change the way the client feels and thinks. Someone from this camp may teach a client the downward spiral technique, which enables them to test their own irrational thoughts against factual evidence and looks at the effect of holding extreme, catastrophic beliefs on their emotional stability, substituting more rational thoughts for the extreme ones. Or, they may take them through distress tolerance exercises where the client takes pre and post exposure-to-the-experience readings of distress levels while doing something such as shopping or going shopping without buying anything, called a non-shopping trip. They log distress readings over the next several days and then learn that their distress dissipates and that they survived.

CBT uses a long list of very serviceable tools and tends to appeal to those who value using their powers of reason to change things. All of this can be done collaboratively and productively with an experienced CBT therapist. The early research indicates this approach is effective about 70% of the time with the treatment group, and at eight months' follow up, those in the 70% group were still happy with the results of their treatment. However, independent evaluators reported subjects were still living with more clutter than the average person, and still had residual behaviors related to hoarding.

Rapid Resolution Therapy ™

As I start to write this section, I can almost hear my fellow therapists out there, "Okay, you've mentioned this method a couple times now, show me some techniques to use." And that's understandable. Therapists are always on the lookout for good techniques. Unfortunately, I can't because the method isn't taught or absorbed that way. It is experiential through and through, meaning it is learned through immersion in the different uses of language and the unique concepts about how to do therapy that Dr. Connolly teaches. Under his guidance, we take turns portraying typical client situations and then take turns being the therapist to get the "client" clear. In real time, going with what's presented, we practice learning to stop the mind from doing what isn't to its advantage and shift mind toward what's beneficial and possible, or we watch how Dr. Connolly does it.

Most therapists were initially trained by sitting in a supervisor's office, at a distance from the client with someone who had never met the client, going over our case notes and remembered responses, after the fact. In RRT trainings everyone is in the client's presence together, and everyone reads moment by moment what is going on for the client, how the piece develops, and how the therapist is playing it. It's a refreshingly different way to learn therapy, more like a music camp, where you learn by playing a certain kind of piece with your instrument, get corrected, and then play some more, until your sound and your versatility is good, or at least a lot better than it would've been had you stayed home!

What I can give all readers is a sampling of what I've learned in RRT and from other sources and have you look over my shoulder as I have applied it to hoarders.

Traumatic Grief

If I'm right about traumatic loss and frozen processing of grief being at the root of most hoarders' problems, then that is where I want to insert myself. I believe that all the cognitive and behavioral disturbances we see are the outward manifestations of the mind misfiring. The mind locks into an assumption of unending loss and abandonment, and the feeling that one is trapped there for good.

What's called the self-state in psychology hasn't shifted, hasn't updated to the present and gotten the good news that the loss is no longer happening. This grief is frozen in its original intense state, and is immediately tapped into when hoarders are challenged to let go of a cherished object or animal. The object or animal is kind of like the cap on a bottle of carbonated soda that has been shaken up. The minute you remove it, you not only threaten another loss, but you release the full contents of the bottle.

But let's back up a moment and put all this in the context of normal grief. Recent research and writings such as that of George Bonnano, a professor at Columbia, who wrote *The Other Side of Sadness*, emphasize the idea that normal grief is an oscillation between two phases. Times of intense emotion with thoughts centered around the loss alternate with times when thoughts turn toward adaptation and look forward to life's next chapter, and feelings are less intense. There is now a consensus around this concept of grief, and it is a change from the stages of grief model that dominated the field for years.

For most, the waves of this oscillation rise higher during the initial weeks and months, but recede naturally through time. As mentioned earlier, my hunch is hoarders don't oscillate, or at least not adequately enough to process the loss. The deep limbic structures of the brain, where intense emotion, sensations, and imagery reside are cut off from the hippocampus and prefrontal areas of the brain, whose job it is to sort and store data and make chronological sense and a coherent narrative out of our experiences. The hippocampal and prefrontal functions are interfered with during trauma, put "off line" as it were. One implication of this is that hoarders never develop a healing narrative or get to put losses into context with the rest of their lives. It just sits there as unintegrated pain.

Looking through another lens, we come back to Jon Connolly, who teaches that grief becomes frozen for a variety of reasons such as: a belief that the death or loss should have been prevented; that someone is to blame; the death or loss was shocking, sudden and/or unexpected; something is incomplete or should have been said or done and now there is no chance of doing so; or there is a feeling the loved one is still suffering or dying. Any of these beliefs can get the brain to lock up and malfunction.

What happens next, Dr. Connolly suggests: "The mind attaches value to what is threatened. The person feels that the relationship with the loved one is threatened." Therefore, the older parts of the brain keep sending a signal to do something about it and to get the threat or the suffering to stop. The mind enlarges and lights up the last disturbing image of the loved one, similar to the way you can take an ordinary photo and make it look more vivid and brighter with Photoshop or a similar utility on a computer. We see them as if they are still hurting or dying somewhere.

While doing this, the mind also blocks off access to positive feelings when thinking about the loved one, blocks off the organizing context of other episodes in their life, or having had nurturing experiences with this person. These experiences are the only thing we ever really get to keep, but having them blocked makes us conclude we've lost them. The profound pain and suddenness of grief creates a massive illusion—that we have lost the person, and that they have ceased to exist. Our five senses and limited perception give us a false read on the picture. Their physical form has transformed, to be sure, but they have not ceased to exist, any more than water ceases to exist when it goes from liquid into gas or the sun when we can no longer see it at night. But with the brain operating in compartmentalized mode, we have no way of knowing it. This is exactly what people report. It's as if they cannot feel pleasure when remembering their loved one, that they are far away or not there anymore, as if they've lost them for good, or that they might still be suffering somewhere.

One of my colleagues, also out of the Rapid Trauma Resolution tradition, Courtney Armstrong, has written a beautiful little book called *Transforming Traumatic Grief* (available on her website http:// www.transformingtraumaticgrief.com).

In it she uses this knowledge and backs it up with modern research that has shown people do much worse with grief when the loved one is seen in the mind's eye as fuzzy, far away, or lost for good. People do much better when they can be helped back into imaginal connections with the loved one and turn the feeling of the relationship from "absent supporter to supportive presence." She has a number of exercises designed to do just that, so grievers are not left with a frozen picture of an actual death scene or a loss, but the internalized reality of a continuing connection to all of the loved one's life and that person's influence in their lives.

Dr. Connolly taught us the solution is two-fold. We have to eliminate the idea that the loved one has stopped being. And, we bring the participant into connection with the loved one.

Earlier I introduced Chester, the hoarder who interviewed with me on public radio and whose home had been unsuccessfully remodeled by his ex-wife and daughter. In the first couple of sessions getting connected to Chester, I remarked on his two Dobermans, Rock and Coco, who were always with him. As he grew to trust me, he opened up that there had been a third dog, Merlin, who had died about a year and a half prior. In our first visit he shared about the devastating effects of his divorce, his best friends moving away, and ultimately his daughter (whom he raised as a single parent) leaving home. But he did not share about this, his most recent and devastating loss.

Chester lets his dogs in and out through a chain link gate that protects them from the street. It turned out one day that while hauling something from his van into his house, with both arms full, he inadvertently left the gate ajar without securing the hasp. Rock and Coco were already inside the house, eagerly awaiting their treat. But Merlin nosed open the gate and bolted off across the street and through the adjoining blocks. Chester got into his van and searched frantically but couldn't find the dog. Later that night, a neighbor came by with the sad news the dog had been hit by a truck and picked up by Animal Services for emergency treatment. Merlin never made it, but died in the back of Animal Services' transport van before Chester ever got a chance to say good-bye. Chester described this as his psychological last straw. From that point on he gave up. He let mail pile up on the sink, quit sweeping or cleaning, ate out of cans, and let wrappers, cans, and containers lay where they were dropped.

I had a solid connection with Chester, so I began by establishing a model of where I saw him heading—not sad, but being social again, with a home he was proud of. There was no conflict about this; he really wanted it for himself. He picked a strong symbol, an oak tree, and we did some things to accelerate and deepen that. One of the things that unlocks unconscious strength is the creation of a model—a robust, sensory-based picture of the participant self-functioning and well again. Then we have the hoarder choose a symbol for it, which "speaks" to the deeper structures of the right brain.

I deepened and intensified this for him by having him hold his symbol in his mind's eye while breathing in and then out more slowly than he normally would. You can do this at home with any goal you want to reach. Just create the symbol for the change you desire, breathe in, then out. As you breathe out, let your eyes close. If your mind wanders, you will see that you become aware it has wandered off somewhere, and that's the signal to bring your awareness back to your breathing. You just gently bring it back to your breathing pattern and your symbol. Just continue like this for 1-3 minutes and open your eyes. You will likely notice you accessed a place of relatively deeper comfort, relaxation, and peace; but also a sharper level of awareness. If you now bring your attention back to your symbol, it is very likely to show up as if it's in Hi-Def—sharper, more vivid, with more colors, or maybe even closer to your face. We know mind automatically reorganizes and optimizes itself, and heals when in this deepened state. It is not that you will anything to happen or go into it with agenda of what is supposed to happen. You just breathe and watch your symbol.

I brought Chester fully back into the room and talked to him for a bit about the mistakes the mind makes when there is a trauma, and how the data about the experience gets mixed up with the actuality of it happening. I explained how the mind loses its sense of time and place. To the old brain, (which we humorously call the "goat") if it thinks a threat is going on, and the mind can think of the preferred action, something else you would have liked to have done (the structure of guilt or regret), then goat says, "Go ahead and do it!" and "What are you waiting for?"

I told Chester how this tendency gets very exaggerated, especially in sudden loss where we tell ourselves it shouldn't have happened, that someone was to blame. It keeps hammering away with this request to do something to make the threat stop until it understands a) the event is no longer in existence or b) it's out of reach (one is no longer able to change or influence it).

At this point I asked Chester to close his eyes, take a couple of breaths, and go to his place of deep relaxation again, and I said something like the following:

"And so take a moment, and be aware of your breathing again, how with each successive breath you let go of air. Air that you don't need. And things in your body that you don't need are instantly transported out. You don't have to plan for it or work at it, your mind just knows how to work with your body and take care of you and is always doing it, running that program in the background. And when you breathe out you are making room... room to take in that which is good and fresh, and light. Just as the light the sun pours into a plant, light pours into you, and it's just taken in, incorporated, so that you are filled up with good things that make sense, that make life better and nourish you in many, many ways....

"But now notice.... as you take in these good things… how you may sense something else, something you already know about… and who knows about you.... He's right here with us. He's already letting me know he's happy...happy to see you… and he's way past excited that you're clearing this up and that you're already getting that he never left.

"You've been missing him, but he hasn't missed you, because he never lost you. You've been blocked from him because of the way things happened that day, but he's never been blocked from you. He's wondered why you've been so distressed, cocking his head, perplexed... but right now he's happy. He's been right here all along, your trusty friend. And see how he's all right? He's not showing up here with any fear of you or distrust in you, and he's letting me know that he still loves you deeply and he knows how you love him.

"He's showing up in the light. And he's in that light that is pouring into you, even now....more, and more, and more. And, you already know what I am about to say...that he couldn't do it any other way, couldn't do other than want **you to be Ok, now,** like he is, and to reconnect to you and the love that the two of you share. And to let you know that you can never lose him; he's as close to you as your own breath.

"In a minute I'm going to be quiet and you'll feel a sensation...maybe a lick, or a breath. And you'll get a message. Go ahead...now feel it and listen for it."

I was quiet for 2-3 minutes as Chester let big teardrops fall from his upturned, smiling face, as his barrel chest took in full, slow breaths and finally let out a deep sigh. He came back into the room, into normal awareness, and reported that he knew that it was all ok. His beloved dog was not suffering and didn't blame him. The whole incident was over. He told me that he had loved dogs his whole life and that they give their owners their whole heart, only asking for protection and love in return. He sensed his dog Merlin felt that way still, and could never be in doubt about their relationship and that the move through the gate that day had been Merlin's own doing. It's just what dogs will do. Chester's voice was steady, neutral, and quietly reflective throughout.

When I visited Chester two weeks later at his home, he had cleaned his entire kitchen area and a dining area that had formerly been stacked eye-high with all manner of used or worn out furnishings and tools. He made a strong statement that he was, "coming out of it" and that he was, "on the road to getting his life back." He said this with a solidity and conviction I had not heard in his voice before.

It is now about six months since I first met him. He has kept those areas clean and has almost totally removed the immense piles of stuff in the other rooms in his house. He is planning for a total industrial-strength cleaning of his home, once the floors are cleared, which our Task Force has arranged through a private company. With this in mind, he has already put in a nice used leather sofa that will be the main piece of his new living room. He started volunteering at the local animal shelter without any suggestion from me, and without any urge to adopt or bring more animals home. He told me he is doing this for the purpose of making a contribution to animals' welfare and possibly meeting new human friends. He is enjoying cooking for himself in a clean, organized kitchen and looks forward to the day, not too far off, when he'll be able to host his first get together. All this has transpired within six months of the session above, after seven years of intense hoarding.

In final reflection on a treatment such as this, some readers, out of their own belief systems, or therapists, out of concern for their appropriate role, may take exception with talking about a deceased person or pet as present and in the room. I am comfortable with it. But I want to be clear, I am not in the business of conducting séances or conceptualize what I was doing here as that. I do feel I was unblocking the barrier Chester's mind had erected to feeling positive feelings, the frozen image his mind had transposed on their entire relationship by feeling responsible and not getting to say good-bye, and trauma's way of setting up the illusion that his beloved chum was gone for good.

It would've also been okay to talk about the one who has transitioned as having a continuing influence on the hoarder in terms of personality or legacy, with traits that will live on, and of the hoarder's connection with that person as experiences that they have not in fact lost and that nobody can take away. I've learned the bond does not cease with bodily life. There continues a conversation in the here and now that the hoarder can draw on as a tremendous resource. Science is now backing us up in the efficacy of reconnecting people to their loved ones like this. They recover better over the long run, and I am way into that for its own sake.

Relational Traumas

Let's keep in mind that all traumas are not obvious at the time in terms of their final impact. When someone goes through the windshield of a car, sees someone killed, gets assaulted or sexually violated, the magnitude of trauma, with a big "T", makes sense to us. But there are many other types of trauma, such as being humiliated or rejected at a young age or experiences of invisibility or abandonment, where one felt their needs, even their existence, didn't matter; experiences of implied violence, bullying or terrorization. These, and many other life experiences, could be called trauma with a small "t," but their effects may show up later and just as intensely. (For more detail, please go to my blog and see "Trauma is in the Eye of the Survivor" at www.markchidley.com.)

When the frozen grief is about how one was treated in one's family or by others, the frozen grief can be just as intense, but its character changes. The wound isn't about a physical death, but what's called a violation of connection. A violation of connection has been defined as the experience of abandonment or betrayal at one's greatest point of need. If this wound is not met with an emotionally attuned response, you have a trauma with a small "t" that for some may resonate in relationships all their lives.

Recent studies of human relatedness, like the research of Susan Johnson, hold that attachment injuries and violations of connection can be just as severe as any other kind of loss. Our old brain understands them as such because the old brain doesn't distinguish between types of loss. In addition, from a survival point of view, the pain makes sense. In the wild if you're alone or abandoned your life expectancy just went way down. The old brain switches on saying, "Do something about this, now!" And the switch can stay on decades after a caregiver is dead and the actual betrayal or abandonment is "out of existence." The switch can stay on, for example, in regards to an ex-spouse, even though they may have re-married and moved on, "out of reach," as it were.

But if that family member or person is still alive, or there is still a possibility of relatedness, frozen grief obviously doesn't stay where it is in the sense of feeling the person is gone forever. Hoarding can become an unconscious attempt to get the person or the relationship back, out of the perpetual threatened zone. When frozen grief is about someone still alive, then hoarding behavior can take on the quality of a maneuver or a message.

It has been observed that many hoarders seemed to live with an unquenched need to be appreciated, and that they may use their hoarding to send a message: "See, I really don't need you." I think the message could also be, "Here I am, come get me, come show me you care." Under these circumstances, hoarding becomes about being noticed, being appreciated, or even ultimately being rescued. But because it is so repugnant, it serves the hoarder's other purpose, to keep others at arm's length, because others just may hurt you again. So there are two intentions that work at cross-purposes to each other, creating a stoppage in the flow of emotional energy, resulting in even more depression. To invest emotion is to direct emotional effort at something , and when the ongoing investment is either counterbalanced by another intention or put into something that won't respond to your energy, depression is the result.

One hoarder I worked with, Iris, comes to mind in this regard. Her house was full of stuff, mostly items under $10 in value, which she amassed in buying sprees from various bargain stores. A sufferer with adult ADD, it took several sessions for me to connect with her and really understand where her thoughts were taking us. It was always back to her dad and sister. Years before, in a grim replay of the Cinderella story, dad had favored the sister over Iris with a gift of a large sum of money. This came at a time when Iris desperately needed corrective facial surgery and had no means to pay for it. The father knew about this need, so the injury was stinging and deep. Iris grew up painfully shy to avoid eye contact with anyone, lest she catch their eyes focusing on her face. She ruefully vowed to never ask her dad for another cent, but instead started buying like crazy and stockpiling goods.

She remained exquisitely sensitive to any contact she had with her father and was vigilant for repeats of the original dynamic. With sobs and tears she told me of offering to bring the beans to a rare family Fourth of July picnic. Her father called her up the night before, telling her to leave all covered dishes at home, her sister had already done all the cooking necessary. The emotion in my office was raw, out of all proportion to the slight.

What I did was move her in the direction of a new model self, one who while still related to her dad in a biological sense, was no longer tied to him for validation or sense of adequacy. I saw her strong, free, enjoying her life, saving up for her own cosmetic surgery, realistic about her dad's limitations, her mind no longer able to get even the slightest bit upset. I saw her open to new, nurturing friendships with people who would respond to her, and connecting in new, exciting ways with her husband of 30 years. That was my intention for her, and strongly conveying it, I began the connection. Checking for conflict, I determined she really wanted this, too.

After some deepening techniques, I had her alternate between her symbol—a rainbow—and an episode in her life where she really was strong and capable, where she had done something remarkably altruistic, an episode that had made her happy, proud of herself, and feeling worthwhile for helping another. I then had her look back on the younger self, from that vantage point. As we shuttled back and forth, this younger self progressively got the news that she would move on in her life into other things, including holding down a very responsible job and moving into a stable and loving marriage. This took several re-workings until she saw the critical incident as a way station, a place she would ultimately move through and around, on the way to the older and wiser Iris.

In RRT we tell a lot of stories meant to be overheard by the subconscious. I told her about two girls both confronted with the same obstacle as they were hiking in a dense forest along a park trail. The first girl came across a downed tree that completely blocked the path. It was a giant tree, so old and tall that its long branches formed a thick network that was all but impenetrable. She nevertheless worked her way in among these until she was right next to the trunk and pushed on the tree, and pushed, but it didn't budge. She pushed on the rough bark until it cut into her skin, until her hands were bleeding and all her arm strength was gone. Then she cursed the tree and beat on it with her fists, and starting to cry, kicked at it with her full fury until her shirt was snagged and torn and the soles of her shoes separated down to the heels. She finally dropped down beside it with her head in her hands, completely undone.

A second girl came up the path and spotted the tree. She didn't do anything at first, but looked and looked and thought about it. Then, not wanting to get tangled up with the tree, she worked her way around, through the soft needles and blanket of leaves on the forest floor, until she came all the way back to the main path about half an hour later, on the other side of the tree. She went on her way, humming one of her favorite tunes.

Iris nodded her understanding and left my office beaming.

I wish I could say that was the end of it, but unfortunately her father inflicted yet another wound and Iris slipped back into her agony of rejection and went out and bought some more. But we headed off the relapse quickly, and have stuck with it. Each time we meet she is getting stronger, getting her headlights off her dad and turned outward, back on the path that lies in front of her. She is now working with me on a plan to donate items to worthy causes and clear her house for good.

Will Chester and Iris stay shifted and clear? So far so good. I like working this way and I hold the conviction that the deeper part of our mind, with its immense power, when reached with a language it understands, can make profound changes relatively quickly, with an efficiency we do not fully comprehend.

I do not infer here you should go out and just apply these techniques, regardless of the context. For many readers, these specific examples will not fit for you or your hoarder. But I mention them because sometimes a lot is possible in day-to-day interactions. Particularly if you are looking at the situation through clear eyes, and you don't get hypnotized by what the hoarder thinks is possible.

There are many ways to help a person re-establish a loving connection with someone they've "lost." It can be as simple as watching them pick up an object, muse over it, and asking them what thoughts the object brings to mind about their loved one. If it fits, you could even ask them to write a letter to that person and then have them write for the person, answering in a separate letter. You could initiate going through old picture albums and have the hoarder describe the photo of a favorite memory, having them recall the event with all the sensory data and detail they can muster. Then use it as a springboard to have the hoarder tell a living story, in the present tense, of how that person still influences them or how their spirit still shows up in their life now. Courtney Armstrong's book has many such interventions. Bit by bit, your hoarder may start to update to the present and de-emphasize having objects or animals as substitutes for what's becoming internal.

VII. Following Up

The team assembled around a hoarder is like a tide that comes in, sometimes with as many as 15-20 members, who as each perform their roles, then recedes, with team members exiting the scene one by one, until only the visiting therapist or perhaps professional organizer, or, of course, family, is left coming by on a regular basis.

There are four key pillars that find a consensus in the hoarding literature that form the scaffolding of a recovery and wellness plan. I'll say a word about each.

1. Building a social network and relearning social skills.

While the tide is in, the hoarder has plenty of new "friends." But they really aren't friends in the usual sense, but professionals doing their jobs. And therein lies a trap. As they accomplish their role and leave for good, the hoarder can feel alone and abandoned again. This is why many authors emphasize working on social skills and even planning for a social event before the project is completed. Find out where your hoarder keeps his or her telephone notebook. Make a list of folks they could still connect with. If they have a computer and aren't too intimidated by learning how to use social media, introduce them to Facebook or Google Plus. Be careful, though. The idea is not to replace one addiction with another, but to reach out to people and create a reason to get out of the house and meet face to face. Or, host a coffee get together in the newly cleaned house.

Most hoarders have a significant level of social anxiety. For years they've imagined their every sneeze is being watched and judged by the masses. The trick here is to have them approach a social situation when they don't have to. This is how I did it with one hoarder. I learned of his love of reading in three areas: mystery, travel, and cooking. I called the telephone reference department of the local library system and got their schedule of book discussion clubs. Such gatherings are also found in the community section of local newspapers. Many churches, senior centers, or park and recreation departments also have similar listings. We looked at the schedule together and he chose the mystery-lovers discussion.

I then gave him the assignment of going into the library branch several weeks before the first meeting was to be held, just to pick up some brochures, and casually meet some of the staff. His assignment was simple: 1) go in and ask some general questions and 2) don't die.

Librarians are very happy to give timely information and they love to resource readers, making them among the world's easiest people to talk to. By doing the assignment at a time he didn't have to, he avoided focusing on having to perform or worrying about others' judgments in the actual situation, and just naturally practiced his social skills. His sense of discovery and empowerment was palpable, and this is usually the case for anyone who has purposely hidden from others and only imagined the worst for years. A month later, attending and taking part in the mystery club's discussion was a piece of cake for him. The hoarder learns making friends happens quite naturally if you just observe what others are doing and ask questions, or express interest around things held in common.

There is also a counseling principle called "grading" at work here. I have them start off with something relatively easy and where success is almost assured and then work up to something a little more challenging. These interventions work because the subconscious figures anything you go out of your way to avoid must be dangerous. That's where they've been. But the converse is also true. Anything you go out of your way to get near to or do must be safe. By doing it at a time you don't have to, subconscious starts to flip the activity into the "safe" category. You can take situations such as the above to the next level, say, like walking up to a group of people you have nothing immediately in common with but who are preoccupied with something they have in common with each other. Now that's challenging!

Like approaching a group of firemen who are kibitzing as they start their day at your local fire station. Those guys always seem to be out front on the apron or by the engines, shooting the breeze as they organize their duties for the day. The hoarder might ask about the proportion of calls to get cats out of trees or little old ladies up who have fallen versus calls for real fires. Or you might have them ask about the wear and tear on a fire engine in a fire and the amount of special maintenance that is needed afterward. It is not really hard to think up questions to ask about someone's vocation and most people like answering, even if the questions aren't all that on target or informed. Even if they are busy or don't feel like talking, the socially anxious person learns they've lived through it, and that's the point. Their heart didn't stop and the world didn't come to an end. And if they don't connect, it doesn't mean they are being rejected, simply that others were too busy to talk or didn't feel like connecting just at that moment.

Socializing doesn't happen 100% of the time (the inflated idea socially anxious people have about others' success rates), but if you keep trying it, it does happen a great deal of the time. It's a good lesson to learn or re-learn. And it's just the way it works for everybody.

2. Replacement Activities

Finding out what the hoarder liked or enjoyed doing before all the hoarding started is a good first step. The hoard itself, a veritable personal time capsule and collage, may give some clues. Professional clean up experts have said they can often trace back to what the hoarder was doing or what activities they valued by looking at the bottom layers of the oldest piles. The hoarder's bedroom often represents a special place of sanctuary and they will sometimes have stowed away not just junk, but items of great personal significance that remind them of who they once were. The idea is to sift out a connection to who they could be again, providing the activity does not lead to more hoarding and is a truly healthy replacement.

For instance, I noticed that Chester had the shelving in a secondary bedroom filled with out of date photographic equipment. Developing trays, enlargers, everything he once needed as he, characteristically, dived into his hobby with both feet. Much of this stuff is now obsolete, with the conversion of photography to digital platforms. But nonetheless, he once loved it, so I took it out and dusted it off for consideration.

I live in one of the most beautiful spots on earth for photography. Southwest Florida, with its bird sanctuaries and breathtaking seascapes and sunsets, attracts pros and amateurs alike from all over the globe. I challenged him to sell off or donate some of the old equipment and get himself a newer camera and "just get out there" again. He knew so much about it; I wasn't worried he'd bump into another aficionado and be at a loss for something to talk about. This idea caught his interest and before I knew it, he was bargaining and bartering with someone who mentioned she too had kept some of her old equipment but still went out whenever she could. This of course could lead to a new friendship or joining a club and starting to find purpose and acceptance again.

Volunteering helps hoarders get outside themselves and give something back. They feel good when lending someone else a hand. Hospitals, animal shelters, churches, non-profits, and many other organizations have volunteer auxiliaries and are always looking for new recruits. A word of caution is necessary here, however. As an addiction counselor I've many times witnessed the "born again" phenomenon, as a new group member dives right into to someone else's life before their own recovery is really stabilized. They get overextended taking care of someone else, which distracts from having to shore up all the out of control spots in their own lives. There is usually a protective mentoring system of more veteran members in AA or NA to head this off, but such recovery assets are a new territory in hoarding.

To put this issue another way, people in early recovery are still vulnerable, whether they know it or not, and sometimes attract predators, others whose lives are in chaos, who would gladly take someone down with them. Last time I checked, drowning people don't do a real good job of saving other drowning people. In my experience, only as a person strengthens and lengthens their time in recovery, can they take on more stress and discern boundaries more accurately. You may have to work with a hoarder to weigh choices and monitor with them the amount and depth of involvement at first.

This follows into something near and dear to me: the resources and activities of a local Hoarding Task Force. With the recognition of hoarding as a disorder, Task Forces are popping up around the country, more common in larger urban areas, but increasingly in midsize and smaller communities, as well. Where I live, we have put together a local Task Force on Hoarding, which is now entering its second year. As we mature, our role in the community is expanding from educational resource and clearing house to consultation service and connective link between agencies. There are many beneficial micro activities in this development that can provide recovering hoarders a place to plug in, if they so desire.

For instance, we are currently organizing a support group that will no doubt evolve from the parent group into several offspring support groups that will meet in different parts of the county. We have a lady who is several years in recovery and stable enough to take on a leadership role and whose experience makes her a natural model and authority for those just coming out of the shadows. She will likely anchor the support group arm of the task force.

Others help us get ready for events such as a recent community seminar that was put on, through staffing various positions, including phone calling, publicity, interagency visits, directing traffic and hospitality, etc. Hoarders have a wealth of professional and life experiences that you want to find out about and tap into. But again, I digress. The support groups' primary purpose is meeting to provide peer support and direction for hoarders reaching out for help. They will no doubt develop some autonomous functions apart from our Task Force, as we all go forward in "The Cause."

I believe in a buddy system, or better said, an early intervention team. Part of our recovery program is assigning every hoarder to construct a list of three people that they would call if they felt in danger of slipping backwards. These are hand-selected people who care about them and would, if necessary, answer a call even at night. The team might include an understanding neighbor, a counselor, a social worker, a pastor, a non-hostile family member, or another hoarder who is stable in their recovery.

The team of three might have different roles. One might be the "sounding board," the one the hoarder talks most easily with, who could help them sort through whatever was going on, identify any triggers, and gently remind them of their goals and commitments. Another might be their "wheelman," who would come and get them out of the shopping mall before they spent the limits of a credit card or filled their basket with stuff. Another could be their "mover and shaker," the one with the muscle and the will to help them clear that last room and to encourage them to quit procrastinating before it gets too overwhelming. The roles can be as varied and individual as the hoarder's needs. But it is the hoarder's responsibility to brief each one on the way they might be needed and then these team members make a one-year commitment to respond in kind if they are called upon. I have found the early intervention teams can take shape as part of a larger support group's activities. They are metaphorically like the ski rescue teams that go out for people in the Swiss Alps. When they get the alarm, they just go, no questions asked.

3. A continuing relationship with a knowledgeable therapist

All therapists come from a primary theoretical orientation that they turn to most often to organize their thinking about how to help. That's to be expected, as is the fact that most good therapists add to this as they develop, getting further training in their primary approach or expanding to learn other approaches that help them with different populations of clients. Whatever the approach, you want to make sure, as I mentioned, the therapist is willing to make home visits, has done substantial reading in the hoarding literature, or gained some practical experience, and finds themself comfortable and wanting to work with hoarders. You don't want someone right out of school (unless they worked with hoarders as part of an internship) or who is winging it because they got real interested in the

TV show. You certainly don't want a therapist who is struggling with hoarding themselves, and is helping others to distract from their own issues, as has been known to happen. We don't want the drowning trying to save the drowning.

We can't go into all the issues dealt with because the range can be so extensive, but obviously experience with severe anxiety and loss is a must. I covered some things earlier under mental health services in Chapter 4 about credentials. I would recommend the therapist be familiar with and up to date with the various medications used to treat anxiety, depression, attention deficit disorder, and obsessive compulsive disorder, and who has a good working relationship with a psychiatrist willing to team with them on the case.

There is a huge debate going on about the over-use of medication to "treat" psychological conditions. I favor the use of therapy to get at root causes, whenever possible. But I'm enough of a realist to recognize there will be times when the right medication is necessary to get a person stable enough for therapy to work.

From the hoarder's perspective, your therapist will probably be the most consistent and enduring member of your team. This is your go-to person who will accompany you on your journey of breaking free. You should feel their unconditional positive regard and warmth and sense their skill. The therapist's job is not to always make you comfortable, but to help you see, feel, and react to things differently. Your home becoming more functional again is one measure of this relationship working, but not the only measure. You should start feeling like you're getting the old issues that have bothered you in better perspective and like you're reconnecting with your life and other people again.

If your therapist came on the scene through the idea of someone else, or the function of an agency, please give him or her a chance to help you. If the session takes place in your home, please respect it as a professional meeting and make use of it as the valuable opportunity for growth that it is. You don't owe your therapist anything, other than the fee they may charge, but if you commit yourself to honesty and matching their effort with your own, you will arrive at a new life, free of hoarding.

4. A framework of self-discipline and organizational skills

There are many skills that can and should be part of the hoarder's recovery repertoire and which help them stay on track. Here is where the input from a professional organizer, a coach, or a therapist who can teach life skills really pays off.

Far more than just reorganizing a closet or a space, a professional organizer can help decide on a system or set of guidelines that a hoarder can use on their own permanently. I agree with Matt Paxton, it's not ultimately about bins, labels, or cool filing systems. Helping a hoarder stay clean is about learning to process the items that come into the house and staying on top of daily and weekly self-maintenance duties that make life livable.

For instance, a common suggestion is a system of containers in the garage or utility area into which a hoarder can easily separate out what gets donated or recycled, separate from trash. Trash is emptied daily. Recycle or donation bins are put up by the door and are taken weekly to their appropriate destinations, so recyclable materials and packaging, which seems to show up in every corner of modern life, are not allowed to build up.

Personal experience makes me biased toward a hazardous waste bin, as well. When my father died and I had to empty out his home and prepare it for sale, I found numerous cans of gasoline, shellac, varnish, stains, paints, bottles of pesticide, rat poison, and lawn care products, as well as old batteries. One thing about Dad, he was always prepared for any job, and so cheap he wouldn't throw out a tablespoon of something he might use sometime in the future, even if it meant creating a wall of stacked cans. He wasn't a hoarder, but still had a wall I had to tackle.

Harsh chemicals and poisons can break down over time and present a dangerous situation either through coming into contact with them or their fumes, and can actually eat right through metal and plastic containers. I spent hours with a mask, Clorox, scrub brushes, scrapers, rubber gloves, and a pressure cleaner getting these off the concrete so the house could sell. Hoarder's homes are full of such hazardous materials and my general rule of thumb is if any supply hasn't been used in a year, it's time to take it to the hazardous waste dump. Your county waste management office can tell you where the nearest one is located. The one-year test is, "Have you touched it or used it? If not, out it goes." This is not a bad rule to follow about other general items as well (not jewelry or valuables). A hoarder may protest they may need it, but point out they can always go out and re-purchase a $5.00 supply, which compares well to storing volatile material, using up valuable space, or risking a hazardous spill.

There are various methods for streamlining paper and reading materials. Junk mail doesn't even make it into my house. It goes right into the paper and cardboard recycling bin kept on the outside of the garage. An area of a counter or desk can be a zone where an immediate sort is done of the rest, such as personal correspondence, bills, and other mail. You can buy stackable desk basket sets at any office supply store which will allow you to further sort items into three categories: 1) that need urgent attention 2) that need attention within two weeks to a month or 3) need attention sometime in the next 3 months. Most business and banking cycles run their correspondence, invoicing, and due dates within those time frames. Outside that time frame, for things that are truly important, you are going to get a reminder on it anyway, so into the trash it goes.

A rule for reading material is if it is over a week old, it gets recycled, regardless whether or not it has been read. Only handle it once. If you need some part of it, clip it out and throw away or recycle the rest. The idea is the hoarder learns to deal with paper according to its true priority level, and doesn't let it build up.

Something as simple as a household chore list, with chores or repeating house maintenance items divided into daily, weekly, monthly, or seasonal categories can keep one on the straight and narrow.

If a hoarder is living with others, it may be time for a sit down talk about defined personal spaces and agree upon rules for each one maintaining their own. Parts of a vanity, bookcases, and closets can be divided and responsibility allocated in a way that makes living together make sense. I was recently visiting a long-term residential drug facility, a home-like environment that was set up just this way. Everyone had daily responsibility for their own bed, desk, and closet area. And everyone shared responsibility for common areas, like bathrooms, living room, and kitchen with their name written on a list for scheduled cleaning or pick up of those areas.

Posted laminated notes can remind a hoarder or others they live with that there is a place for everything or an expected routine in a given room. Who has not seen a sign posted in the coffee lounge or break room reminding people to turn off the coffee pot and wash it at the end of the day, put all items back in the refrigerator, and throw all trash away? Anyone who has ever been part of the scouts, group camping, or the military remembers there is an intensive group clean up at the end of each day. Everyone takes an area, usually very small, and makes sure it is picked up and cleaned for use by the next group.

Even if a hoarder lives alone, if they can get into these routines, they build self-esteem and pride. The recovering hoarder on our task force, Kathleen, has a personal rule of never leaving her house until her bed is made and all dishes in the sink are cleaned and put away. What she gets in return is knowing she can bring any visitor into her house at any time of the day and be proud of its appearance.

The In/Out rule is most helpful to those who need to control excessive acquiring. I recently saw In/Out being taught on a TV program for parents to help them teach kids to make good decisions, who are always bugging them about more toys. In/Out means whenever something new comes into the house, something of equal size must go out. For adults, this insures that stuff already there has to be used up, traded, sold, recycled, donated or trashed before something new comes in to occupy its space. It means ultimately that there is always the same approximate volume of stuff in the house.

Hoarders who acquire compulsively can go shopping with a coach or a sturdy friend who will walk them through a set of tough questions before any purchase or acquisition is made. Here is a compilation from various sources and experiences: "How many of these do I already have, and is that enough?" "Do I need really need it, or just want it?" "Do I have a specific plan to use this item within a reasonable time frame?" "Can I afford it right now, or (even more to the point) "Where's the money going to come from?" "What won't I be able to pay for this month if I buy it?" "Do I have enough space for this?" "Could I get it again if I found I really needed it?" "Does bringing this home fit with my current values and goals?" "How will bringing this home affect a person I care about?" "Will it make my life better or worse?"

These new questions, routines, rules, and tips get a hoarder out of bad habits and automatic behaviors into thinking for themselves and maintaining a sane lifestyle for a new reason: because they are worth it.

Follow Up As a Study in Human Being Rather than Human Doing

Realistically, change can be one step forward, two steps back. Hoarders have a well-ingrained relief system that they may slip back into and only relinquish by degrees. And if we are honest about it, helping doesn't always go smoothly. There are many factors that can lead to an impasse for hoarders, many triggers that can cause a relapse. Here are a few I've seen:

- Their problems with maintaining attention and prioritizing things may put them crosswise of a city code enforcer who then must act, making the authority the hoarder's focus, not their own goals for change.

- Their need for a companion or to find worth through being needed or rescuing can lead them into repeated offences and bring Animal Control and/or law enforcement down on them.

- Their elaborative thinking or extreme ambivalence may drive them to clear an area one day, only to sneak out the next and get more of their favorite things, to the consternation of family and those helping them.

- Maybe an enabler or other forces conspire to bring in an extra animal; they will say "yes" when they should say "no".

- The emergence of past traumas may surface by finding an old photo, or possessions of a loved one, triggering real or imagined deprivation or abandonment connected to an episode which no longer exists.

- Current family has a way of stirring the pot, of providing more drama at just the wrong moment, taking the hoarder's eye off the goal.

- Or perhaps the hoarder is still sending a message, trying to squeeze appreciation or recognition out of someone, and then acts out when they don't get it.

These are just some of the developments that can cause a momentary hiatus in the plan or an outright regression. We must always remember how much a person's neurology changed for them to get to a place where it seemed normal to live with 50 cats or in rooms piled to the ceiling with stuff. And how difficult the road back might be.

I agree with the Harm Reduction philosophy that says it's best to see recovery as a journey and any progress as a step in the right direction. And it's wise to know when to step back, to do no harm, such as when denial or just plain being overwhelmed makes progress impossible. When setbacks come, they are seen as expected. Because of the sheer complexity in attempting to change an entire lifestyle, we can't foresee every twist and turn that might come. Sometimes we can only wait for the momentum of a situation to tip back toward change and listen for the hoarder's motivation to return.

For families, this is the hardest time. Unless you are forced to take extreme measures, the best you can do is fall back on connection and letting the discrepancy build along with verbal skills for highlighting it. At the right time you might ask a hoarder how they are doing with their cramped space or the decline in their health. You might inquire if they get frustrated not being able to find things, or if they are worried about being out of money for more necessary items. Are they stressed about what the landlord or neighbors might do? You might suggest they look back on how they were five years ago, in general, and ask themselves if they are better off or worse? The idea is to keep a laser beam on the difficulties that start to accrue along with concern for the pain that is caused, looking for a point of leverage where the hoarder might develop a willingness to talk about a goal or getting help.

I was taught to never put any kind of treatment failure back on the client, but frame it as a lack of skill or knowledge on my part. We don't want to further poison someone whose own thought process is likely doing a bang-up job of it already. When setbacks come, expert helpers pay attention to the overall scaffolding of recovery, do a walk-around inspection to find which pillar gave way, or which one needs more strengthening. Hope is a huge part of the hoarder's recovery mediated through the quality of being that helpers manifest at such times. I never forget that whatever is going on, a hoarder is learning about relationships from me. And for them, it is ultimately about getting past loss, distrust, and learning to relate again. Whether a goal is accomplished or not, I can always leave them with a strong impression that the connection I share with them matters, and that they are a real person to me.

Epilogue

"Roll the stone aside," Jesus told them. But
Martha, the dead man's sister, protested, "Lord, he
has been dead for four days. The smell will be
terrible."

Jesus responded, "Didn't I tell you that you
would see God's glory if you believe?" So they
rolled the stone aside. Then Jesus looked up to
heaven and said, "Father, thank you for hearing
me." Then Jesus shouted, "Lazarus, come out!" And
the dead man came out, his hands and feet bound in
grave clothes, his face wrapped in a head cloth.
Jesus told them, "Unwrap him and let him go!"
John 11: 39-41, 43-44.

Somewhere out there, a very sad person is
rolling to the edge of her mattress, swinging her feet
to the floor to begin another day. Only her feet don't
touch the floor, but a layer of plastic water bottles
and old food containers that crinkle and pop beneath
the weight. There are bugs everywhere. It is

unsanitary. The blinds and all windows to the world are shut tight, and even though it's morning, the house is dark and dank, like a tomb. She is someone's mom, someone's aunt, or someone's grandma, but it has been months, even years, since anyone came by or called. A deceased husband's picture is covered in dust, but still visible across the room on the dresser. A reminder that once there were people, a reminder that she once had a life. It is garbage pickup day. Her high point will be digging through neighbors' trash bins or maybe the big dumpster out behind the Super Target, looking for any treasure to soothe the pain.

Who will break into this world? Who will be sent, and who will go? Who will keep coming, even on the dark days, when the hope of change seems far, far away?

If you decide it's you, you won't be alone. There are many of us starting to care. The air you breathe in will be the air we just breathed out, the air of healing, breathed out by your brothers and sisters who have gone in, just like you, not because of how much they knew, but in spite of how much they didn't know. They went in because they cared. We are all together there with you. And the rays of our light will entwine together and become a beacon of hope, strong enough to break through the darkness, strong enough to lead one more soul back into the light and the life they were meant to live.

Sources

Armstrong, Courtney (2011). *Transforming Traumatic Grief.* Artemecia Press.

Bonanno, George (2010). *The Other Side of Sadness: What the New Science of Bereavement Tells Us about Life After Loss.* New York: Basic Books.

Connelly, J. (2009) *Clinical Hypnosis with Rapid Trauma Resolution.*

Jupiter, FL: Institute for Rapid Resolution Therapy. Training Manual Re-Issued, 2011.

Frost, Randy and Steketee, Gail. (2011). *Stuff: Compulsive Hoarding and the Meaning of Things.* Mariner Books.

Frost, Randy, Steketee, Gail, and Tolin, David. (2007) *Buried in Treasures: Help for Compulsive Acquiring, Saving, and Hoarding.* Oxford University Press.

Frost, Randy, Steketee, Gail. (2007). *Compulsive Hoarding and Acquiring: Therapist Guide.* Oxford University Press.

Frost, Randy. Information shared with the Lee County Task Force on Hoarding at an informal briefing at Florida Gulf Coast University, February, 2010.

Johnson, Susan M. (2002). *Emotionally Focused Couple Therapy with Trauma Survivors*. The Guilford Press.

Miller, William R. and Rollnick, Stephen (2002). *Motivational Interviewing*. Second Edition. The Guilford Press.

Paxton, Matt. (2011) *The Secret Lives of Hoarders*. Perigee.

Tompkins, Michael A. and Hartl, Tamara L. (2009). *Digging Out: Helping Your Loved One Manage Clutter, Hoarding, and Compulsive Acquiring*. New Harbinger Publications, Inc.

For more on the initial research and writings about hoarding, you can visit the Hoarding of Animals and Research Consortium website at www.tufts.edu/vet/hoarding/index.html.

Rapid Resolution Therapy and Rapid Trauma Resolution were founded and developed by and are both trademarks of Dr. Jon Connelly and are used under license. All references herein refer to the actual teachings and techniques he invented for use with various populations and which are learned in Level I, Level II, and Level III RRT trainings. For more information go to www.cleartrauma.com.

About the Author

Mark A. Chidley, LMHC, CAP is a licensed
mental health counselor and certified addictions
professional, practicing in Fort Myers, Florida. He
received his education at The University of Iowa,
Princeton Theological Seminary, and the University
of South Florida. He was one of the founding
members of the Lee County Task Force on
Hoarding. In private practice since 1997, he is
certified in Rapid Trauma Resolution (2010) and
now specializes in the clearing of trauma as well as
treating hoarding disorder and training and
supervising other professionals as first responders.

Made in the USA
Lexington, KY
17 January 2017